Refuge
under
the Boot

REFUGE UNDER THE BOOT

Talvikki Manninen

VANTAGE PRESS
New York / Washington / Atlanta
Los Angeles / Chicago

To my son, Harri

FIRST EDITION

Copyright © 1985 by Talvikki Manninen

Published by Vantage Press, Inc.
516 West 34th Street, New York, New York 10001

Manufactured in the United States of America
ISBN: 0-533-06515-1

Library of Congress Catalog Card No.: 84-91447

Contents

Author's Note

I have written my story not because I feel I am different from other war refugees who have gone through some horrifying experiences, but because I am one of them.

Maybe this book can be a forewarning to future generations so that they can be better prepared for the catastrophes a future war would bring.

Foreword

Sixteen years had gone by since I lost my four-year old son, Harri.

Some of those years full of starvation, misery, and fear I spent as a refugee in the middle of the chaos of the European warfront.

Would I ever find him again?

Was he still alive, and if so, could I ever be able to make him understand what earthly power had torn us apart?

Those were the thoughts that haunted me constantly during my flight as a refugee, from place to place, from one country to another.

Refuge under the Boot

CHAPTER 1
The Early Years

My beloved, brave little Finland, squeezed between your neighbors, Sweden and Russia. Growing up in your lovely forests, knowing nothing about that giant Russian bear that could swallow you with just one yawn. Never for one minute did I dream that I would ever leave you, flee from you. I played on the sandy shores of your Lake Saimaa, and plunged into blue billowing waters in the twilight of the midnight sun. I romped around on the majestic cliffs of your roaring and glittering Imatra rapids, and sang Klemetti's impressive patriotic song:

Oi kallis Suomen maa . . .

(Oh, my beloved Finland)
No other quite so dear on earth,
As this my native land. . . .

I enjoyed you during those years of peace and laughter and cried with you during the war. Those were the precious years of my youth and I will never, never forget you.

I am here at a massive wooden table which Norman made, writing in my little notebook. Our house, a two-story wooden structure which we built with our own hands, has been our paradise for several years now. It sits 3500 feet above sea level, right above the town of Kernville, California, just five minutes from Lake Isabella, where we go for a refreshing swim or for fishing. We can see great pines and live-oak covered slopes from our scenic balcony and hear the Kern River with its rushing rapids below us, as red and yellow rubber boats go bouncing down at great speed. Here one can fill the lungs with fresh country air and find peace of mind.

Here in Kernville I am solid, comfortable, and warm. This is my resting place, my sanctuary. Sometimes I feel as if God is making up for all of my suffering during the first half of my life, sitting here, surrounded by the silence, my mind wanders back to those years now long past. I can think about the world I once knew with all of its love and hate, misery and happiness.

Around me are pictures of my family. There in front of me is a picture of a small five-year-old boy in a navy blue sailor suit, smiling sweetly. That's my son Harri, whom I lost for so many years. He's now a grown man, tall and handsome, with a life of his own and a family to rear.

Across the room sits a picture of a beauty queen in red velvet robes and shining crown. That's Regine, who died in a car accident ten years ago, before she really had a chance to live a full life. She was only twenty-three.

Another picture shows a pretty girl in a song-leading outfit, looking happy and healthy. That's Christel, the child who barely made it through the chaos of war, now happily married and with children of her own.

And last but not least there is Norman, my companion all of these years. He was able to graduate from college after the war, and he has always worked hard to help his family, the girls and me. We couldn't have done without him.

But this is today. Now let me go back and tell you the whole story, and how it all began.

When I was two years old, my mother and I moved to a small town with cobblestone streets called Raahe, in middle Finland, on the west coast of the Gulf of Bothnia. She had a teaching position at the seminary and we moved there to live with Aunt Sikke, father's sister, on Ranta street.

Aunt Sikke was very small and thin, and had her dishwater blonde hair in a bun that looked like an onion. She was an old maid and very religious, and she read the Bible out loud every night. I didn't understand anything she was reading but it sounded pleasant, almost like music. Then she would play the organ and we would all sing.

Mother had taught me my first song:

Vaik' olen pieni heikkokin,
en pelk ää kuitenkaan. . . .

[Although I am small and weak,
I am not afraid. . . .]

On Sunday morning Mother lifted me on the table at the church and I sang it to the congregation; then Mother had tears in her eyes as she hugged and kissed me.

She was so sad those days. My father had died a few months earlier. The dreaded typhoid fever had swept our country after the victorious war in 1917 when Finland gained her independence from Russia, which had dominated my homeland for years.

I was told that my father, Harald Julius, had been a handsome man with light brown hair and small, gray-blue slit eyes, full of laughter. "Exactly your eyes," Mother said, looking at me. As a doctor of Philosophy and a director of a teacher's college in Joensuu, middle Finland, he had always worn a stiff collar and a goatee. In Joensuu he met my mother, Hertta Ingeborg, one of his students. They fell in love and after her graduation married and moved to a little Nordic town named

Kajaani. An idyllic rapid river, Ammakoski, ran through the town and there was a picturesque, old, white wooden chapel inn the middle of a green park, with colorful flower gardens. Father continued his career at the Kajaani Seminary and they had four children in this town.

My oldest brother, Elja, also died of typhoid fever, two months after my father, at the age of six. My sister Enni, a fussy and pretty brunette with green, shiny eyes, and my sister Lea, a small and delicate blond curly-head, had been born only one year apart. I, Talvikki Marja, called Vikki for short, made my entry into the world in December, two years later. Being only one year old when our father died, I had the privilege of staying with mother while my sisters were placed in the homes of relatives, Mother missed my sisters very much, but she could not take care of all of us while working every day for our living.

Mother was beautiful. She was slender, healthy, and intelligent, and she had the bluest eyes in the province of Karelia. She could laugh and sing like a lark and play the piano too, and she dressed like a fine lady in feathers and furs. Yes, she was a lady.

Aunt Sikke took care of me while mother taught school. It was not an easy task for an elderly woman to run after a lively, vivacious child. She was kind and good-natured, but I learned to take advantage of her and ran away every time she turned her back.

Her home and its surroundings made a very interesting place to romp. The house was a small, one-story, white one with dark green window sills and doors, and there was a high ladder in front of the porch. One day I saw a man dressed in black coveralls and a black top hat, carrying some brushes and other paraphernalia on his shoulders, climb up that ladder and disappear behind the chimney. I thought the man looked very interesting and so I decided to investigate. I climbed

4

right after him and before my poor Aunt Sikke realized I was gone, I was sitting on the roof beside the chimney-sweep, happily chatting away and unwilling to come down for any money. It wasn't until Jussi, the chimney-sweep, reached into his pocket and handed me a piece of candy that I decided to follow him down. Jussi and I became very good friends, and every time I caught a glimpse of him I ran to him and collected some of the candy he always had in his pocket.

I learned very well how to con people for goodies. Often Aunt Sikke took me for a walk into town or to the church gardens which were filled with the most gorgeous red and white geraniums and where I fed the squirrels and birds. Once I tore loose from my aunt and ran into a store nearby, curtsied, and said breathlessly, "My name is Vikki." That was all. My small, gray-blue slit-eyes were full of laughter, and they and my blond curls did it. I got my candy every time from then on, too.

Aunt Sikke's house was very neat and tidy. There were hand-crocheted, white tablecloths on tables; a huge, old brown rocking chair in one corner of the room, where Aunt Sikke always sat knitting or reading; and also a high, dark hutch, a cabinet with very interesting old porcelain plates and cups and other decorative china. And then there was the old organ, a dark, shiny brown one with attached bench and bellows that squeaked so strangely when I stepped on them.

The house had wonderful fenced yard full of birch and pine trees and lilac bushes in glorious blue or white, and there were patches of yellow daisies and red geraniums. In her yard I could climb fences and trees, feed Fifi, the red-eyed white rabbit, and chase the black cat, Musti, with the white spot on his nose. Musti was my favorite, but there were other cats and dogs in the neighborhood that belonged to my Wonderland. I made the animals all mine and followed them. I climbed on roofs and trees. I fell down, got bumps and pains, a broken collarbone, and bleeding wounds, but I survived.

One glorious Sunday in June, in the late afternoon, Mother and Aunt Sikke took me, then four years old, to the sandy beach of the Bothnic Sea. They told me it was Juhannus, the Finnish Midsummer Festival, celebrated each year. As we climbed down the endless steps lined with green jasmine bushes with small white flowers, a new world spread out before me. There was sand and sea as far as one could see. With eyes wide open and hanging on to my mother's hand, I watched the fires, large and small, burning all along the beaches and on the islands. People dressed in national costumes of various colors were dancing and singing folksongs. Some fires were in the middle of the water on home-made rafts, while rowboats and motorboats as well as slowly moving sailboats moved in circles around them. The flames leaped up and down looking like fiery plumes of roosters. People kept feeding the magnificent bonfire and the smudge flickered and sputtered when the frigged wind bit into it, and the music from the boats played on and on. My first *Kokko* (fire) celebration left a deep impression on me as I gazed into a new world of wonder.

Oh, how I loved nature! Often mother took me for long walks through forests. They cover three-fourths of Finland and are the main source of her wealth. Deep green forests of pine, spruce, and birch, full of squirrels that we fed and colorful birds of all kinds that we mocked. We picked blue violets and wild pink roses on the way. We sat on the rocks and sang and sang. Mother had such a clear, high voice. She taught me one little Swedish song which became very important to me in later years. Thinking of it gave me courage on many occasions. Hand in hand we sat there and sang:

> *Skiner sol, hördes åskan gå*
> *Lika glad är jag ändå*
> *Gar det väl, visst fröjder det mig*
> *går det illa, nog reder det sig.*

6

[Whether the sun shines, or thunder rolls
So happy I will always be,
All goes well, I will rejoice,
Though all goes wrong, 'twill come out right.]

You see, Mother was partly Swedish, and we spoke both Finnish and Swedish at home.

I was almost six years old when we took a trip to Lake Paijanne in the famous lake district in central Finland. It had rained a week but that Saturday morning I was awakened by the first golden rays of sunshine in my eyes. The air was so fresh and cool and we set out on our trip in a small country train. I enjoyed sitting by the window and taking in the glorious sweep of the vivid green fields with patches of white daisies and bright blue cornflowers. When it would change suddenly into thick forests of tall pine.

Here and there we passed a winding river or one of Finland's sixty thousand lakes, and as we approached the central lake district, it seemed like the whole area was splashed with lakes and a network of canals, rivers, and bridges. Oh, what a breathtaking beauty it was! With my eyes wide open I tried to take it all in and wished I could fly like a bird over this phenomenon to be able to see and appreciate the whole setting, unrivaled in its beauty. This must also have been a paradise for fishermen. One could see them everywhere in their boats, pulling in their nets, or standing on cliffs casting their lures, and watching the blasts of wind stir the sea and the bluish waves chase each other about the bay.

We took a sightseeing trip in a small boat and circulated from island to island through canals and under bridges, and then stayed overnight in a small hotel on the waterfront. We woke up in the morning to the peculiar clarity of Finland's summer mornings, which are so invigorating. This trip was like a wonderful, unforgettable dream to me, and through this and many others like it, my mother taught me to love my beautiful fatherland.

Soon after our journey to Paijanne there was a program at the seminary in which I took part. Mother had made a gorgeous dress for me for the occasion. I still remember the white lacy summer dress with pink lining and a large, pink bow on my blond curls, and the new white shoes. I danced around as if on clouds and gave a curtsy and a smile to everyone. As my mother played the piano I sang: "*Se orava se hyppeli varvullaan.* . . . [A squirrel was jumping from tree to tree]." There was endless applause, hugs and kisses. The thrill of that applause never left me, and who knows if that wasn't the beginning of my musical career?

Aunt Sikke had been a teacher of Home Economics in her younger days, and she was very artistic and handy with any sewing, knitting, and embroidery. She taught me how to make potholders, sew doll clothes, and often we surprised mother with many handy items. She also taught me to play her organ. She pumped the old-fashioned bellows for me because I could not reach them, and we performed for Mother, who laughed and laughed thinking the two of us a funny-looking duo.

And then the day came. It was in the autumn when the yellow leaves started to fall slowly and gently from our birch trees. Mother came home from school and said "Vikki, my darling, we are going to get a new daddy for you and your sisters, and we are all going to move to Sukeva. You are going to like it there. The house is by a beautiful lake in North Finland. And your new daddy is a nice man." I didn't understand why we had to have a man when she had me and I had her, but anyway she insisted on it.

That fall we left Raahe and Aunt Sikke cried at the railroad station. There was a hug and a kiss and then mother pushed me into the coach of an express train that was ready to leave.

One of my dear friends, I called him Nami-Seta, came running to the train carrying a red wooden basket full of candy and handed it to me just at the last moment before the doors were slammed shut and the train was ready to roll. His goodbyes were drowned out by the din of the locomotive. "Goodbye, Aunt Sikke; goodbye, my black Musti-cat; and goodbye, my precious childhood memories."

CHAPTER 2
A New Family

It was three years after my father's death that my mother remarried.

Our stepfather, Vaino Kalle, was of medium height, a competent, ambitious man of thirty, who had brown thin hair, bald in places, and sharp gray-blue eyes that could see through you. He had a friendly face, although he was very quick-tempered, especially after having had a few glasses of "Black & White," which he always had when playing chess with his friends. He was a good provider as a Director of Forestry, and had a fine home for his new family. The greatest impression I had was of the wonderful nursery room he had, with toys for all of us, in one corner of the light green two-story structure.

The house was surrounded by spruce, birch, and maple trees, and bushes with shiny dark green leaves and red berries. From the balcony in the back of the house you could see the sweep of the valley with its vivid green hills and slopes with blue shadows. Nearest to our house, right below the hill, was an enchanting lake with a small island and a stretch of warm, honey-colored sand.

In this lake, called Sukeva, my sisters and I spent most

of our time learning to swim, play water ball, row the boat, and just run and romp on the sand. Many steps led down to this beach where we found the *puku-koppi* (dressing room) and the green boat house with a typical-Finnish wooden rowboat and a fancy—very fancy—mahogany motorboat. Stepfather was good at steering the motorboat and we made numerous trips around the lake and to the green island where we often had picnics and picked blueberries, lingonberries, and various mushrooms.

Kaisa was stepfather's old housekeeper who had been with him for three years, ever since he had bought the house. She stayed with our family for years and years. She was about fifty-five years old, had a somewhat deformed face with droopey, watery, blue eyes and straight gray hair mostly covered with a white scarf. Uncle Vaino, as we called our stepfather first, had a playhouse built for us under a large spruce tree. It was built out of birch lumber and painted red, and every morning Kaisa put some goodies on one of its shelves for us. I knew then that I was going to like her.

The most important item in the new home was a big, black shepherd dog with a white diamond-shaped spot on his chest. His name was Iiro and he was a great playmate when he got to know you, but was vicious to all strangers. After a few scratches and teethmarks which I received, we got along fine. We became friends, and from then on Iiro was my dog.

Mother didn't have to work anymore, so she had more time for the children. My sisters, Enni and Lea, went to school nearby, and Mother and I spent that time together in many ways. She taught me to knit and embroider, and we took long walks in the deep pine forests. In the endless winter we had a sled and skis, and a *potkuri* too, for our recreation. The latter is a sled with long metal runners and a high seat like a chair. It's steered with wooden steering gear. Four or five people can stand on those runners and hang on to the person who is steering. What fun it was to sail down a long, icy hill with my friends. It could be dangerous, of course, but who worried about that?

Stepfather had a riding horse with a long brown mane, called Lisa, and mother rode it almost daily and sometimes took me with her. What exciting fun it was to sit in front of her on the saddle and trot down the sandy roads and over fields! But one day the horse kicked sister Lea on the leg quite badly, and after the doctor fixed it, there was no more riding for us children.

Stepfather also had a reindeer in his stables, a funny-looking creature with huge antlers branching with numerous points and very coarse gray hair. We called him Poro, which means reindeer. I was afraid of it; but one winter when I saw stepfather flying over the drift-covered fence in his red *pulkka* (sled) harnessed to his reindeer, it looked so exciting that I took a chance and sat in his lap for a round of the fun.

Before the year was over stepfather had an offer for a better position at Tainionkoski in the province of Karelia in east Finland, close to the Russian border. We packed our bags and moved to an estate, a white two-story house with fifteen large rooms, in the middle of a deep forest between Saimaa, one of the largst lakes in Finland, and the winding Vuoksi River. Through the high windows in the den and over the second story balcony you could see the glittering rapids of the river. In the winter moonlight the colorful icicles hanging from the roof formed an interesting and beautiful frame for the river below. The house had very large windows with green window sills and a brown hand-carved wooden silhouette of a squirrel decorating each gable. Oravala (Squirrel Haven) was the name given this house, and later they called me the squirrel of the Squirrel Haven because I loved to climb all over the roof and the yellow-green trees around it, and swing from the tree to the balcony, to my mother's horror.

11

The lower level of the house included a large hallway leading to a huge living room, a den-music room with a black Steinway grand piano, a dining room with a large hutch and a long oak table with a dozen heavy armchairs. Stepfather had an office furnished with dark brown leather furniture and a huge bookcase. In the long hallway hung stepfather's hunting gear and trophy pelts. The master bedroom had a dressing room and the maids had their own quarters. But the kitchen was really something. It had a huge stone hearth in one corner, made of field rocks and heated by wood. The one side of the hearth formed an oven for baking bread, and Kaisa and Hilda could bake eight large round delicious loaves of bread at one time, pulling them out of the oven one by one with a long-handled wooden spatula. I remember well the sourdough rye bread, which the Finns are famous for baking, and the *pulla* which is now available even here in the U.S. in some bakeries.

The upper level of the house was more interesting to the children, with its large nursery and playroom, several bedrooms, a bath, and a very interesting attic with lots of things to play with. Besides that, and this was very important to me, one could climb from the upper balcony to the great, black roof, with the help of the branches of a large silvery-leafed tree on the corner. What great fun that was!

The only sad part of our moving was that my beloved dog Iiro was left behind. He had torn the trousers of a neighbor boy and after having to pay a fine, stepfather had had him put away. It was a big loss to me, and I cried for many days.

Of course we had a sauna bath, a typical Finnish one. It was a separate building in the woods behind the house. Some people build theirs of logs, the gallery and dressing room of wood and the pit of field rocks. Many people build their sauna house first and live in it until the main structure is built. For many families it was customary to do the laundry in the sauna and for that we had a great big water pot of iron on top of the fire pit, which was stoked with plenty of wood. To take a sauna bath is fundamental to all Finnish people and they enjoy it at least once a week, some lucky ones even every day. Bathing in the nude is the custom to get the full benefits of the bath, and then we whip ourselves with a whisk of green birch twigs heated in hot water. This makes the blood circulate well. After that we splash ourselves with cold water from a wooden tub. Oh, what a wonderful feeling that gives you. Some people will jump into a lake after a sauna bath or in winter they roll in the snow or take a dip in an icy hole in the lake.

Hilda, a second maid, was a new addition to our family. She was a typical Nordic woman with broad shoulders and a wide butt. She had a big bosom and the darkest brown eyes I had ever seen, and she let me crawl in her bed and hide between her teats many a night when I had nightmares and was frightened.

Then there was the chauffeur, Ville, who accompanied stepfather on his business trips and often spoiled us girls by driving us on our errands, although mother protested that it would do us good to walk. Ville was big and strong with a lot of dark-brown, crinkly hair and he was very humorous and always told us stories. I can remember how he would laugh until his eyes were full of tears when he bought us hotdogs and put so much strong Finnish mustard on them that we had to grin and make faces.

Mr. Tanttu was the riding master who acccompanied my mother and gave her riding lessons and whenever they returned home I was allowed to ride our thoroughbred black horse Maska to the company stables one mile away. Oh, how happy and proud I was able to sit on the saddle and trot through the woods and fields. After a few lessons from Mr. Tanttu I was able to gallop and control the horse. Often I spent time at the stables talking to the horses and I knew them all by their names, but Maska was my pride and joy. He was "my" horse.

In our *porstupa* (entry) there was a large barrel of drinking

13

water with a huge dipper filled once a week by a waterman named Jussi, a kind man who often allowed me to hold his horse while he was filling the barrel. I loved his horse, a light brown percheron named Paula, and as I talked to him he would listen and wiggle his ears and sometimes even neigh to me in answer to my chatter.

Our inside toilet was in a small separate room where a large bucket was placed inside of a wooden bench with a cover. A big bellied, shaggy man wearing a brown leather apron came every other day with his horse-drawn wagon to empty the bucket. We called him the "Honey King" and in our eyes he was a very important man; sometimes we followed him and even rode on his sled although mother didn't like the idea for the odor it left on our clothes.

I was afraid of my stepfather. His violent temper flared up very fast and when his anger was directed at me he hit me so fast and hard with a dog lash that I often fell down. Yes, he was ready to whip us, but after losing his temper he seemed suddenly to soften as if ashamed and would sometimes give me pocket money to make up for it. Being the youngest had its benefits. When stepfather gave us all a spanking, my turn would come last and by that time his anger would largely be spent and I was spared the punishment.

The worst punishment I remember being given, chiefly for being late to dinner, was being sent out to the woods in the dark. Often I sat down on a rock slumped in a helpless bundle and cried, fearing that I'd be attacked by a bear or some other wild animal. I would cry and cry until my mother came to rescue me. My stepfather was the violent, unpredictable ruler, a powerful man; but in spite of the punishments, I loved him, because he was the only father I knew.

Mother was always sweet and kind and from what I remember she seldom took part in our punishment. She was so beautiful in her riding costume of black, high leather boots,

14

black velvet jacket, light gray breeches, red high-collared blouse, and to top it all a black velvet cap with a riding crop in her hand. I was so happy with her and so proud that she was my mother.

CHAPTER 3
My Growing World

One of the unforgettable characters of my childhood was Madam Ritz a Porta, our governess. She was very small and her face looked like a dry prune. We often made fun of her, the way she peered through her horn-rimmed glasses and we copied her rather strange old-maid image. She had been in high court circles in czarist Russia and, during the revolution, she fled from St. Petersburg to Finland. This aristocratic old lady in her early sixties spoke several languages fluently and was in great demand as a teacher of French, German, Russian, Swedish, English, and Italian. Some of our friends were invited to join our tutored language classes and it was as gay a school for me as could be imagined. Madam Ritz a Porta also taught us old English table manners, including grace, and from then on we spoke only English at the table. As a governess she also used our round metal gong to signal the family to gather for dinner and if we girls were late, there was no dinner for us that day. Needless to say, she was very strict.

Music, music, music. Our home was full of it. Mother, a good pianist, and Enni, a perfect accompanist, played the most. Sister Lea and I had to beg to be able to use our grand piano. It seemed it was never unoccupied. Later, Mother, who played Rachmaninoff's Piano Concerto and Liszt's Prelude by ear, accompanied me as well. Stepfather played the violin very well, especially Brahms' Lullaby, his favorite. Mother frequently joined him with her piano. And sometimes all five of us sang in chorus or three of us girls harmonized under mother's direction and sang her compositions. Every time we had guests, my sisters and I sang trio for them, and soon we were good enough to sing in various programs. From that period on, the study of music became my goal.

In my first year of public school, when I was seven, my mother was the teacher. She was asked to take the place of a teacher who took a year of absence due to illness. It was great fun to walk two kilometers to school the first day holding my mother's hand, other girls and boys joining us on the way. Everyone wanted to walk with the teacher and I was very proud to be her daughter. When the class started, however, it was different.

As the roll was called and it was my turn, my mother asked: "What is your name?" I looked around, hesitated, blushed, and whispered: "You know it, mother!" but she insisted on it so I started to cry and was terribly embarassed. My own mother didn't know my name? What would other children think? I refused and was sent out of the classroom.

Later the school principal found me standing behind my classroom door, a bewildered, frustrated, tearful little girl, crushed to think my mother didn't know my name. "What is it, Vikki?" she asked.

An anguished, sobbing voice replied:: "Mother doesn't know my name."

"Well, come now, Vikki dear, I'm sure we can work this out," and so saying she took me by the hand and led me back to the classroom. But the first day of school was ruined.

Once school started I had to wear shoes I hated, the kind with the thick soles and brown high-laced leather tops. Boys' shoes, that's what they were. I was a tomboy, my mother told me, and was very hard on shoes and clothes. I was ashamed of those shoes and stumbled and tripped over them on pur-

16

pose, and told my mother they hurt my feet even though they were comfortable.

From our house a winding sandy road ran through the woods to the paper and pulp factories where stepfather worked. He walked to his office and often I accompanied him there. He was usually quiet and walked slowly, a little slumped, deep in thought. But I didn't mind because my imagination ran wild all the while. In the deepest woods I imagined all kinds of wild animals. I managed to frighten myself with my vivid fantasy and it felt good to have stepfather by my side to keep me safe. On the way back home I always ran as fast as I could. At times I felt I was a horse with a man riding me, a whip in his hand. I galloped like a horse and could almost feel that whip on my back. Once I thought I saw a big, bearded man in those woods, calling me and trying to catch me. I was so frightened I ran in a panic all the way home. Mother thought surely I had been day-dreaming.

Stepfather sometimes took me with him on his trips around the country, Ville chauffeuring us in our limousine. He took time for fishing and hunting along the way and those were great times for me. He hired a boat in some village on the coast or by a lake and we'd go out, the two of us, stepfather at the helm, hanging onto the fishing line while I rowed the boat. He was so strong and handsome with a pipe in his mouth, and I felt he was more intelligent than anyone I knew. We would start at sunrise, in the reddening dawn, when the mild wind was lifting the gray mist and the blue-green waves gently rocked our boat. It was quiet and peaceful with only the birds in the nearby woods for company, twittering and chirping. We were alone, seldom seeing any other people in those waters so early in the morning. Occasionally there was a slight movement in the stillness around us; a bird arrowing from the tree tops, a fish breaking water or the deep croaking of bull frogs. Sometimes stepfather sang, his thin hoarse voice breaking the silence with a favorite Finnish song like "*Sulla on silmat SINISET ja mulla on veden harmaat.* . . . [You have blue eyes and mine are watery-gray]. "He put a special Finnish accent to it so as to make it sound funnier and it was just that. There was plenty of fish available. One needed only to throw out the lure and soon start pulling in one silvery fish after another. Most of the time we caught large pike and perch on those trips, and we kept the fish alive in our boat. Stepfather lifted the wooden plug and filled the boat with water, and the fish swam all around between our feet. We stayed in a fishing camp overnight many times and had fresh fish for our dinner. In the evening stepfather had his whiskey and read his paper while I daydreamed of castles in the sky. On some very cold autumn nights we watched the gorgeous Northern Lights (Aurora Borealis), typical in northern Finland. The whole hemisphere was dominated by flashes of fire-like lights which were jumping and playing to and fro and hissing across the entire arctic sky. It looked like the whole arc had burst into flames. There was nothing in my world then bothering me. Stepfather sometimes read aloud about the possibility of war with Russia, which could be disastrous, but I didn't understand what it was all about and kept on dreaming of pleasant things. Why should I worry when I had my stepfather to take care of me? All I had to do was to behave and do exactly what he demanded. I also went with stepfather to the deep forests in Karelia during the hunting season. Once, on the way there, we saw hundreds of milk cows, and stepfather suddenly turned to me and asked slyly, "Do you know how many cows there are in that field, Vikki?"

"No, I can't count them so fast, Dad," was my answer.

"There are 1,649 cows," he said grinning.

Astounded I asked, "How can you tell?"

"I counted the teats and divided them by four, and the odd number is a bull," he said and laughed and laughed. He was a humorous man.

I enjoyed tremendously the long walks in those woods. But at times stepfather insisted I stay in the cabin while he was out hunting. I didn't mind, however, since I always had my dream world to go to and I didn't have to look at the dead and wounded animals which always annoyed me. This trip he shot a small black bear, a red fox, and a large, colorful Metso bird, which was stuffed with spruce boughs to keep it fresh. The spruce needles add fragrance to the game as well as remove some of the wild taste. At home we had a large black bear pelt on the floor in our living room, and when people admired it, stepfather always told his story regarding the pelt, and it always brought the biggest laughs. He was a great storyteller. It goes like this: "A group of us hunters, Peter, John, and I were staying in a small camp deep in the woods some time ago. The first morning, while the others were playing cards, I decided to go hunting. Shortly I spotted a big black bear. I took a quick shot at it but it wasn't dead, and the bear reared up and started toward me. Quickly I headed for the camp with the bear on my heels. Upon reaching the camp door I stumbled on the steps. The door flew open and the bear in great speed leaped over me into the cabin. 'Skin this one!' I shouted. 'I'll go and find another one for myself.' And this is it."

One of the nicest places in my childhood memory is Rautio-Hovi in the midst of deep, hilly woods about twenty-five kilometers from our home. It was owned by the firm where stepfather worked. The wooden ranch house had one large room with double bunk beds ready for our use anytime. The caretaker family, Mr. and Mrs. Karttunen, cooked and cared for us very well. Sometimes we stayed a week at a time, enjoying the animals they kept there: horses, cows, sheep, chickens, pigs and geese. And the spruce woods were full of wild berries and varieties of mushrooms. The latter we cleaned in the woods and then soaked and salted them for the winter and the berries we cooked into marmelades, jellies, and jams. Our maid Hilda was always with us on those trips, and she was so much fun for us children and such a help as well. In Rautio-Hovi I learned to milk a cow and to round up the horses from the pasture.

A large, shaggy sheepdog named Hippi, became my constant companion. When he was on my heels I wasn't afraid of anything. On one clear, sunny Sunday morning, when Hippi and I were making our rounds, we found a new path which we followed. Over the rocks and moss-covered hills we climbed, higher and higher to the highest point. Oh, what a breathtaking view spread before our eyes. A wide, winding river, the trees in their autumn colors, a small town with a white chapel below. The birch trees shimmered and the pines pricked the sky and everything was at peace with the world. I knelt down on my knees beside my Hippi, and put my hand around his furry neck, and a deep sigh rose from within. What a wonderful place this was! I was glad to be born in Finland, proud to be part of this land, and I felt this land was mine. This day I felt the presence of God!

At the age of twelve, I was full of vitality and laughter and had grown taller and stronger than both of my sisters. My oldest sister, Enni, now sixteen, was a young lady. She was going to high school in Porvoo, a town a distance away from us, and came home only on vacations. As time went by, we younger sisters stared at her full bosom. She was so pretty and looked like a little lady. I wished I would look like that some day. However, Enni seemed to grow ashamed of her development and appeared very modest in the sauna. She tied a towel tightly around her bust so that we couldn't see her bosom. We never dared to talk about those things with each other.

Sister Lea, a serious and frail little girl, then fourteen, was sent to a boarding school in Sweden where she stayed the whole year. I called her my little sister because she was so small and never could protect herself when the neighbor-hood boys teased her and jumped on her. I always felt it my duty to rescue and protect her. Sometimes I overreacted. Once, when a boy grabbed my long braids and pulled me around in circles I struggled myself loose and hit him squarely in the mouth and he ran screaming home to his mother. After that episode his mother and mine had a serious discussion and I was put under house arrest for a week. I could be tough if I had to.

And then my little stepbrother was born. His name was Kai, short for Kari, and he was a lovable and happy lad and became thoroughly spoiled by his sisters and his parents. He grew into a healthy, strong boy and was well taken care of by our governess and by Hilda while mother was away.

Mother was busy directing a choir in our town. She was a chairperson of a woman's organization called Lotta Svard which aided Finnish soldiers at home as well as at the war front. There was fear of war and everyone wanted to be pre-pared, just in case. Mother also organized an orphanage for children. Between all of those duties, plus giving piano lessons and singing, riding, and traveling, she was a busy lady. Yet it seemed she always had some time for her children.

Those were pleasant days at our home. We were a happy family, happy in ourselves and in each other. There were some sweet religious customs. Stepfather said grace, holding mother's hand, and evening prayer was read with mother sitting by us holding our hands. I remember my mother's custom of waking us up every day at seven to do gymnastics on the balcony. That was fun!

Christmas was a special time for the family, of course. We had yearly Christmas caroling tours to hospitals and to the homes of bed-ridden people we knew. In a horse-drawn sled, in our festive red and white dresses and bonnets, while buried up to our noses in fur coverlets, we rode out on Christmas Eve. It gets dark very, very early in winter in Finland, and not many stars twinkle in the black sky. The wind would be puffing snowflakes into our faces, but with the Christmas spirit inside of us, we went out to sing.

On Christmas morning, just when the wintry sun sent its first rays through the clouds, we were out on the road. There would be many sleighs and much jingling of bells. The church was about ten kilometers over the frozen lake. The minister was in his festive robe and it was a solemn and impressive moment for me, listening to the Christmas sermon and the Christmas music in the church with a fresh, green, decorated tree, together with the people I loved.

Back home again, we had our Christmas sauna first, then ran back into the house, barefooted and barely clothed. I often wonder how we got by without catching a chill.

Following the sauna we had to dress up for the delicious and festive dinner, cooked by Kaisa and our faithful Hilda. It was customary to eat as a first course a dish called Lutefish or *Lipea Kala*. Preparing it in those days was a lengthy process. First one bought codfish which had been soaked in lye water for some time and then dried. The fish looked like logs of wood to me. The odor was very strong and they were soaked in water outside for a couple of weeks. Thereafter, the fish, wrapped in cheesecloth, was ready to be boiled in salt water for about ten to fifteen minutes. The fish tasted bland, but with mashed potatoes and a specially prepared white sauce, it was delicious.

This course was followed by ham baked in a bread dough, rice porridge with a lucky almond in it and, of course, dessert, which amounted to a number of home-made prune tarts.

Our Christmas program began later in the evening. The doors to the music room would be opened by stepfather first so that everyone could take a look at the brilliantly decorated tree. This was stepfather's special surprise and he always chose one of the children to help him decorate it. What an honor it was. Then, after last gifts were wrapped and poems written on them, stepfather read the Christmas gospel by Topelius, which we all knew by heart. We then sang Christmas carols. While we sang the first verse of our favorite carol, a Santa (whom stepfather had arranged to come) would arrive. He rolled in the snow and then stomped his feet on the balcony steps. We sang *"Ukko tulla lupa, lupa, lupa, lupa"* and when we heard the stomping we stopped and ran to open the door.

I'll never forget the time when I was about seven years old and still believed in Santa Claus, and a distant neighbor, Emil, was asked to be our Santa. Although I didn't know him well, I had seen his fully split nose a few times and it couldn't be mistaken. What a disappointment. Christmas was never the same.

In my high school years in Imatra, Karelia, I was frequently asked to perform. It was something I loved. I sang, played piano, recited poems, and had leading roles in plays. I even danced soft-shoe ballet. Mother was very proud of me then and was determined to send me to study music after high school. It was also my own dream and desire. Without music I felt like I couldn't fully live. It gave meaning to my life.

During these years mother was fortunate enough to be able to take a long trip to several European countries. I missed her from the moment she left. She planned the trip with a close friend, Katie, and they boarded a ship in Helsinki, taking off for two months.

Meanwhile stepfather taught me to play tennis. We had a tennis court nearby so it was very handy. I had been watching him play with friends for a long time while I chased their tennis balls. It didn't take me long before I was able to play with stepfather. I was given a few lessons by Mr. Martinson during the summer. He came all the way from Helsinki for that purpose. I'll never forget his strange appearance, with his plucked and colored eyebrows, his colored lips, and pointed finger nails. He looked nauseating to me and stepfather said he was "queer." I didn't know what that meant, but it didn't in any way affect my regard for his instructive ability, and I enjoyed having him teach me to play tennis.

Mother's first postcard arrived from Koblenz, Germany. I wanted so much to be with her to see all those legendary castles and art galleries. Until now I had been so involved in my own world that I had had no interest in other countries, so far away. Now I was becoming curious.

Next came a card from Paris. She was very excited about all the art museums, the baroque palace and the opera house, and, of course, the Eiffel Tower and the Arc de Triomphe. It was good to hear from her; I missed her and needed her love and guidance so much.

The mailman, Esko, arrived one fine day waving a letter from mother. With the letter in my hand I ran to my favorite place—the romantic green swing—and opened it. I wanted to be alone to read it, to feel her presence around me. She told of the elegant Monte Carlo where she lost money gambling; about more museums and sights in Italy; and about the exciting city of Vienna. I could almost imagine myself there with her in those wonderful places. Oh, how interesting and exciting the big world was beginning to seem. I wanted to be a part of it.

CHAPTER 4
Mother Dies

One glorious Friday afternoon, in the middle of August, mother was back. I ran to her arms with cries of joy. My beloved mother. I told her how much I had missed her and I hoped she would never leave me for so long. She was so suntanned and happy and full of stories about her trip.

Soon Mother was busy again. This time she was planning a going-away party for her friend Katie, who was going to move to Porkkala, a famous resort near Helsinki. For that occasion mother composed a song, and because it was vacation time and both my sisters were home, she taught us to harmonize it. Her song told of memories of their journey and wished Katie good luck in her new home. Sister Lea, who had learned to play the Kantele, a very old Finnish string instrument sounding like a harp, accompanied our song. In two weeks we were ready to give our performance and sing mother's song. It was a gay occasion and I saw many pictures from her trip, which increased my desire to see more of the world.

In September, stepfather decided I would be sent to a new high school in Iisalmi, in upper middle Finland. That was the school my father had been a principal of several years ago. Enni and Lea were already back at their schools. It was depressing. That month we had a lot of rain and ceaseless winds. It reflected my feelings. Mother was preparing me for the trip. I was numb. I would be leaving home, without mother, for almost a year. It seemed impossible, rude! I had been taught, though, that there was no questioning the decisions stepfather made.

That fall Mother suddenly became ill. A mild appendix attack, the doctors said. She was up soon and packing my clothes, helping me to try on some new dresses our seamstress had sewn. But on the day before my departure she didn't look well and stayed in bed. I sat by her side, my hand in hers, and we sang our song:

Shiner sol
hördes åskan gå
lika glad
är jag ändå

and then there was a last hug and kiss before it was time for Ville to take me to the railroad station. "Be brave, my dear child, and may God bless you," Mother was sobbing. "I'll think of you always." Only stepfather and little Kai were there to wave goodby to me. Soon the train started rolling and I was alone on my way toward an unknown future. Why did he do this to me? I hated to leave my mother and my home. I was scared!

Iisalmi was a small city with cobblestone streets, and the small white houses stood clustered together. A busy little park with swings and slides was located in the middle of town. The high school had several large buildings including a large gymnasium where we assembled for morning prayer. The auditorium with it's huge windows was the only room I really liked because there was a large piano, an old brown upright one, which I could play. And after music, gymnastics had always been my favorite subject. We also had a students' curfew which ordered us off the streets by ten P.M. every night. My room and board had been arranged in the local minister's home. It was a nice, quiet house. I had a small attic room that smelled musty and the four walls made me feel trapped and depressed. I often had nightmares, and I'd wake up in the middle of the night to bedbug bites which made me feel panicky, and I didn't want to be left alone. Both the minister, who seemed kind and had a soft voice that compelled you to be quiet, and his wife, a respectable-looking lady, tried to make me feel at home, but I needed my mother and longed for my home.

As I woke up one cold and nasty morning in the middle of October it was snowing and the ground looked like a white blanket. Nature was still asleep, and it was quiet and still around me. I felt lonesome and desperate. There was to be a performance at school that night, in which I was to recite a poem. I loved poetry and felt prepared. But as I stood behind the curtain that evening waiting for my cue, the principal rushed up to me and said: "Vikki, there is a message for you from your stepfather. Your mother is very ill and you must leave immediately."

I stood there speechless and frozen.

He took my hand and said he would make the arrangements for my trip, and before the night was gone I was on my way.

There was darkness, a hard corner bench on the third-class coach. Here I was, twelve years old, traveling alone toward the sickbed of my beloved mother.

In the midst of cigarette smoke and laughter I saw the pale face of my mother. I sat on my bench wringing my hands as the train pounded its way slowly, oh, so slowly, and my heart throbbed loudly in a race with the turning of the wheels.

Would I be there in time?

In time for what?

My throat was dry and felt as if it would choke me. Hot tears rolled down my face.

How could anyone laugh at this moment when my mother was dying? I crawled behind my coat hanging in the corner and burst into uncontrollable weeping.

I arrived home too late. Mother had had an appendectomy which had developed into peritonitis and there was nothing in those days that could have saved her.

When they took me to the hospital to see her body I screamed. "This is not my mother!" I cried in fear, staring at the face of death. I wanted to find my mother. Where was she?—Where was she . . . ? No one could give me an answer. I felt as though I had lost a piece of myself.

My mother was buried in Krematorio Chapel in Helsinki. At the funeral I sang a famous Finnish song called "Äidin silmat" (Mother's Eyes). Sister Enni accompanied me on the organ. It was one of the hardest tasks of my life. I will never, never forget that day!

CHAPTER 5
An Unhappy Home

Sensing that life was very difficult for me to face alone without mother, stepfather allowed me to stay home and continue my schooling at my previous high school in Imatra where I had studied only a month before transferring to Iisalmi. However, the situation seemed to get progressively worse instead of better. Life in our household during those days was not pleasant, as stepfather's violent temper flared up more and more. He played chess in the evenings more frequently and he and his friends always drank heavily. I hid upstairs on those nights, in my room, feeling alone and lost. "Mother, I have so much to tell you, and I need you to hold my hand." But I communicated my feelings very little to anyone else. I tried to think of our song, *"Shiner sol . . . "* but I couldn't sing it without mother. The smile had gone from my face.

One wintry evening in December, stepfather came home with a little puppy in his arms, a gift for my birthday. It was a beagle, a hunting dog, and I named him Ari. I adored him! Life was not so lonely for a while. He and I became inseparable. I taught him tricks. He was my pride and joy. We ran through the woods togther and went on errands into town. But a few months later, when I came home from school, Ari didn't meet me at his usual waiting place on top of the hill. I called him and searched for him everywhere. Finally I asked Hilda if she knew where Ari was. She only shook her head for an answer but I could tell immediately that something was wrong. I ran to meet stepfather when it was time for him to come home. "Where is Ari?" I cried. He looked at my disturbed face and then with a little hesitation answered: "I sold him to a friend who needed a hunting dog." I thought I didn't hear it right. I couldn't believe he would ever sell my dog, my birthday present, the only thing that was mine alone he took away from me. I didn't understand it and in confusion I ran to the woods, buried my head in my apron and cried and cried, wept bitterly. I knew I wasn't allowed to protest about anything to stepfather so I didn't, but I could never forgive him for that cruelty.

When I was fourteen years old something new started happening at home, something I didn't really comprehend, and it worried me very much.

Early on Saturday morning stepfather started tapping the ceiling of his room with a cane, my room was above his. When I entered, he told me he wanted me to come to his room and to get into his bed. Without hesitation I did so because I remembered when mother was alive, we children often cradled in their bed and it felt so nice. Warm togetherness. But now it became different. As I, in my pink long nightgown entered his bed and crawled close to him and put my head on his shoulder he put his arms around me and pulled my body tightly against his. First we talked about school and music and such, but soon he started to kiss me passionately and slowly lift my nightgown up, rubbing my body with his hands and pushing himself on top of me. I could feel his erection and was shocked and scared and I protested strongly pushing my knees against him with all my might and finally wiggled myself from his embrace. "Please let me go," I cried, but he became very angry. The blood had rushed to his face as he rose to a half sitting position, took hold of my shoulders, and shook me vigorously. Then he slapped me on the face several times, and let me go.

I ran to my room and hid in my closet in terror. For all the good it did. This ordeal happened again and again and I never dared to tell anyone about it. His sexual advances became more and more persistent and eventually he succeeded in his sexual endeavor. What a pity!

Once in our sauna-house I walked in in the nude, as is our custom. Stepfather was there ahead of me. He sat in the steam on the high bench as I entered the room. I turned my back to him and tried to sit down on the lower bench. He commanded firmly: "Come here, Vikki, and sit by me. I want to see if you are growing into womanhood as yet." Those were horrible moments. He stared at me with lust in his eyes and made remarks about my maturity, but when he touched me I ran barefooted and nude through the snowy path home and was very much afraid of punishment. I was afraid of him. Of course, as always, I didn't dare tell anyone of these incidents.

There were an endless number of restrictions in our home, and our upbringing could be considered strict and rather disciplined. But as I grew older these restrictions seemed to get tighter and tighter and any infractions of the rules were dealt with by the blow of a hand or a leather belt. I remember once asking stepfather for permission to go to a movie a couple of miles away. He agreed, but as usual gave me a certain time limit. That night the movie lasted a bit longer than usual and I returned home late, and frightened. I decided to climb up to our upper balcony on the fire rope, hoping stepfather would be asleep and wouldn't hear me return. Just as I thought I had made it, stepfather suddenly appeared, a belt in his hand. He was roaring with anger and started hitting me with it. His blows were so hard that I fell down to the ground and injured my ankle. From then on I was told I could not go anywhere with friends unless I was chaperoned. Was that jealousy or discipline?

There was one occasion when I asked if I might go to a concert, and after he rejected my proposal, I dared to show my disappointment and was summarily punished; when it was time to go to bed and a good night kiss was due, I hung my head and gave stepfather only a quick kiss on his cheek. For this he slapped my face and took hold of my shoulders shoving me against the wall so hard that several of his precious pictures of ancestors fell and broke into pieces. "It is all your fault," he yelled, and his large strong hand hit my cheek. I was then dismissed and confined to my room. Children in our family did not complain or strike back. We were all under his thumb!

Although stepfather had a violent temper there was another side to his character. He was soft and tender, at times. Many times when he listened to some classical music like Tchaikovski or Brahms, his favorite, his eyes were full of moisture, and I remember once when I was singing "Brahms' Lullaby" he was touched as he appeared at the door and said with quivering voice: "You have a lovely voice, Vikki. For a while I thought I heard an angel sing. Promise me this, when I die, you will sing at my funeral." But then again, most of the time, his stubbornness won and it happened sometimes that he didn't give in no matter what. I recall for instance when, on some important festive occasions, the attire was requested to be a black tie and tails, he appeared in a regular suit just to show his authority. What a scandal it caused those days, but he rejoiced. His fancy long, brown Meerschaum pipe was his constant companion whenever he sat down and I can still smell the delicate fragrance of his Amphora tobacco.

My middle sister, Lea, came home from her Swedish school and had been home for a short time when I noticed her strange behavior. I realized something was bothering her a great deal because she ate less and less, became more frail and often just sat and stared into space. I wondered if she was receiving the same treatment from stepfather as I, but we never talked about it. What a shame we hadn't learned to communicate and to share pain. It might have helped us all if we could have. People were saying that Lea was mentally ill, not normal. She walked in silence and clutched her Bible under her arm, looking so intense. Or she sat and read her holy book in the garden, as if searching for answers. I don't think anyone understood her and I guess no one really tried.

In my last high school year stepfather informed us he was

going to get married to a girl nineteen years of age, as old as our oldest sister, Enni. This was a shock to us. Mother had died only one year ago and it seemed to us too early for replacement. The girl in question was a distant relative of stepfather and was a concert violinist. The music, he explained, had brought them together. No sooner had Sonja stepped into our household, when there was a noticeable friction between her and us children. She was used to having her way in every-thing. She was intelligent, gifted, and very strong-willed and she had been a wonder child since the age of thirteen, when she gave her first concert at the Paris Conservatory. When she wanted something she worked at it until she got it. Sonja was not afraid of her husband's explosive temper because she knew from her experience that she could get anything from him after one of their romantic and wild sexual encounters. This we youngsters sometimes witnessed by peeking through a keyhole.

I remember how possessive we girls were about our home and how protective of our mother's artwork. Especially me. If there was any criticism directed at my mother's embroidery or hand-painted porcelain, for example, I was insulted, hurt, and very defensive. The conflict that seemed to grow between us was increased twofold by stepfather's flying into a rage every time he heard us arguing.

The situation became more and more critical. We had all started out on the wrong foot. And to top it all, when Sonja's mother came for a lengthy stay matters became even worse. She told us girls that our house was no longer our home because we were not Vaino's chidren. As far as she was con-cerned Sonja now owned the house and ruled it. According to her we had no longer any rights. Worst of all was what happened when sister Enni came home on vacation and took part in our arguments. She was strong and tried to defend our part of the story but in the middle of it all stepfather jumped on her and pushed her out of the house. She fell barefoot into a snowbank. Enni was the first one of us to leave home. Needless to say, stepfather was the king and ruler in our household. A word or incident against his will made him lose his temper completely and caused chaos in the entire family circle. Nevertheless I respected and loved him.

CHAPTER 6
A Wedding

I first saw Jorma shortly after my high school graduation. He was stepfather's cousin and he came for a visit to our home. When I saw him pushing his bicycle up our steep hill I thought he was one of stepfather's business companions. I had been deep in thought, sitting on my green swing in the garden and I looked up when I heard him call hello. He was a nice looking man, I thought, slender, of medium height and with nice blue eyes.

"Are you Vaino's daughter?" he asked. "Yes, but who are you?" I answered. He told me that he was stepfather's cousin and that since he now worked at Kymmene Bruk, nearby, he thought he'd come and visit his relatives. He seemed pleasant to talk to and he seemed to consider me an adult, not talking down to me as did any other men I talked to. I learned that he was a graduate engineer at a paper factory and an ambitious man.

When stepfather arrived that evening, he took Jorma to his room where they sat playing chess and drinking Black and White. Jorma stayed overnight and when he was ready to leave he held my hand for a minute and said what a pretty girl Vaino had. I snatched my hand back as soon as I could.

Stepfather replied with a comment I have never forgotten: "Well, maybe so, but don't you know that all pretty girls have no brains?" He then gave me a look that confirmed his feelings. It was a comment I had heard before and had come to believe was true. In fact for years afterward I wondered how I accomplished all the things I did when I was a person with so little brains.

The summer went by and I occasionally saw Jorma at our house. Once stepfather took the two of us for a boat ride, and Jorma talked of his life. He seemed such a lonely man to me. He was thirty-five years old and had never been married. He didn't appear to have a girlfriend either. I enjoyed talking with him and felt as if he were a kind uncle. That is what I called him.

Sister Lea, still terribly depressed, remained very isolated and confided in no one. She just walked around alone. She couldn't even sing anymore. Couldn't stand any kind of noise. Once when I played a Strauss waltz on the piano, thinking it might give her a lift, she became irritable and made me stop playing. She called it "sinful music." She slammed the door behind her as she left the room. Needless to say I was confused. There was a great deal of quiet suffering, it seemed to me. There was so much we didn't dare talk about or didn't know how to talk about, we didn't seem to be able to help each other.

When the leaves started to fall in September and the soft summer winds changed to cool autumn storms, my stepfather made an announcement, he was going to make some changes. He had accepted a new position as a director of a large wood company on the West Coast, and the family would be moving from Karelia.

Sister Lea had been committed to a mental institution. Sister Enni was going to stay in Ebenaeser College in Helsinki until her studies were finished. Stepfather strongly suggested to me that I ought to marry Jorma. He had discussed the marriage already with Jorma and told me it was a wonderful chance for me to be able to marry a prominent man like Jorma. I tried to argue with him, pleading that I wanted to study music more than anything and that mother had always wanted me to be a teacher of music. But, not even the fact that I was only sixteen seemed to make a difference. I found myself being persuaded. Not for a minute did I think to rebel, run away. I guess I had learned to be a pawn in stepfather's chess game and had come to accept it as my fate. The only consolation I found in getting married so early and to a relatively strange person was stepfather's promise to pay my way through music school. It was to be my wedding present. "That will be wonderful," I said and thanked him.

There I was in the middle of preparations for my wedding, but, there had been no prince who awoke me with a passionate kiss from my childhood into a mature woman. There was more fear than happiness and excitement about living with a man for the rest of my life. Of course I loved Jorma as my uncle, he was stepfather's cousin, but I didn't think of him as my lover. I had been afraid when touched by stepfather, and I wondered if Jorma would be like him. I knew nothing of sex, nor of sweet romance and the tender kisses of which young girls dream.

The wedding bells were ringing and stepfather gave me away at the altar. I was dressed in a white embroidered wedding gown with a pink satin sash around my waist and my bouquet was baby roses and orchids. Jorma wore the usual black tuxedo.

When I took Jorma's arm for the procession I noticed how much he resembled stepfather. I was startled by the realization. Congratulations followed and a dinner dance at our home with the usual formal speeches and the wedding waltz for Jorma and I while everyone applauded.

I played my role well, acting happy as a new bride should.

But where were my thoughts? They were far away. They reached out for mother. I wanted her with me, to calm me. I wanted to hear our song, to feel safe. We left the wedding guests and boarded a train for Tampere where Jorma had rented a cottage on an island owned by his well-to-do parents, at Nasijarvi. Bodily contact was not so bad as I had anticipated. Love would come later, I thought, as I had heard people say. And making love was a duty in marriage.

The days flew by while we fished, my favorite recreation, and we took long walks in the deep green forests, and we tried to become better acquainted. We had stayed at the cottage for just two days when we received an invitation to a dinner at Jorma's parents' summer cottage on the same island. During our conversation my mother-in-law angrily criticized stepfather's handling of our marriage affairs. (I had not been told that stepfather had made all arrangements for my marriage without first consulting Jorma's parents.) Furthermore, there were some nasty remarks about my lack of a dowry. I had come into the marriage empty-handed. Needless to say, it hurt me tremendously to be openly attacked and scolded. Things were far beyond my control. When I told Jorma later that I was hurt by all the criticism he commented that his parents had the right to object to Vaino's typical bold and rash behavior.

As time went on I felt increasingly that I was an intruder. I felt my in-laws were inconsiderate of me and considered me unfit to be a part of their snobbish mode of life. I heard more than once that I was too young and immature to be a suitable wife for Jorma. Alone in our bedroom I faced the mirror one night and attempted to assess myself. The face in the mirror belonged to a totally bewildered young girl. I promised myself then I would be strong and grow up to please Jorma. Maybe then, I would be accepted into his family. I had to be strong because I didn't want to be destroyed like poor sister Lea.

Jorma was back at work a week later, in Kymmene Bruk. He was well-liked, smart and successful. We were busy making our rental house as comfortable as possible. I wanted our home to be cozy and neat, our love nest, if possible.

The building we lived in was a wood structure in the middle of a group of similar houses, all of which were surrounded by small flower gardens. Jorma had a housekeeper, Liisi, who continued working in our household. She was a pleasant, snub-nosed, middle-aged woman with thick, masculine arms and legs and her cheeks were round and pink. There was no question about her being able to handle any kind of a household, and that was just fine with me because I had no experience in cooking and baking. The only thing left for me to do was to take care of the flower garden which I enjoyed to the utmost, in part, I suppose, because it had been a favorite activity of mother's.

Kymmene Bruk was strictly a Swedish-speaking community. But although I spoke the language fluently, having learned it from my mother, who was born in Sweden, I soon found out I wasn't favored in this neighborhood since I spoke Finnish in my home. I tried not to care about their world and I didn't want to be like them one day, snobbish and condescending. For years there had been tension between the Swedish and Finnish communities in Finland, and each believed their language and culture to be superior. The Swedes had a great deal more of the capital power and for that reason considered the Finns poor and without culture.

My mother respected the Finns and their culture and spoke Finnish fluently, although her first language had been Swedish. She and my father wanted Finnish spoken in our home.

I remember my mother telling me of a time when my father had been a student at the university years before and had been part of a large number of students who were protesting the use of Swedish as the official language in all colleges and universities. There were protests made and outcries heard all over the nation, and many people, including my father, changed their family names to ones of pure Finnish origins. I believed as my father did that the Finns were not inferior.

There was a beautiful, black grand piano in our living room, and I spent hours practicing my playing and singing. Jorma was involved in many social events and that left me alone a great deal. Sometimes I sat alone until the early hours of morning while he played cards and chess and drank at the club house. It wasn't easy for a naive seventeen-year-old to understand. At moments like these I would think to myself, is this a price I must pay? Stepfather got his freedom to start a new family and a new life. But what did I get? A chain around my neck. Mother, I need you now more than ever. life. But what did I get? A chain around my neck. Mother, I need you now more than ever.

It wasn't too long after we were married that I knew there was something growing inside of me. I would have a baby of my own. After Mother's death I had had very little that I could call my own. Now I would have something that would be mine to keep, my own child. Nobody could take it away from me. Not ever.

I rejoiced. The baby surely should bring Jorma and me closer. Little did I know that our home at Kymmene Bruk was to be only a temporary one. Jorma informed me one day that we were going to move to Helsinki, where he would have a better paying job and a private secretary which would make him more prominent. He was all for that. He never discussed any plans with me. I suppose he felt that someone as naive and ignorant as I was didn't need to know. Somehow he began to remind me so much of stepfather, especially when he had been drinking, and then it seemed the fear I had had in stepfather's house was following me. Sometimes I waited for him until early morning hours while he was drinking at the club and when he arrived he would flop himself fully clothed on his bed. I was terribly upset and cried until morning and prayed to the Lord for help. My mother had taught me drinking was an unforgiveable sin.

As moving preparations got under way I began to anticipate Helsinki with excitement. Our capital city with it's music schools, the Musical Intitute and the Sibelius Academy, to name a few. Maybe I would get to study music as I had been promised. That was all I really wanted now, that and my baby.

CHAPTER 7
Harri and Lea

In the middle of January we made our move to Union Street in central Helsinki. It was a freezing cold winter and there was a great deal of snow. The snowdrifts piled up on the streets making them sometimes impassable. The snowplows worked day and night. The severe cold nipped our noses and bit our numb faces and the intensive, gusty sea winds forced us to often walk backwards, into the wind, as we went from the railroad station to our apartment nearby.

Our home was on the seventh floor of an ultra-modern stone structure. It was a sunny and comfortable home of five rooms with large windows in the living room facing a lovely little park below. Next to the kitchen was a small room for Liisi, whom we had taken with us.

Jorma had bought some new furniture which was already placed in the apartment. The rest was coming by train. After everything was in its place I knew I was going to like it. I felt that this was my first real home since Mother's death.

Jorma started his new engineering job immediately, so I had time to get acquainted with the city. I would go down to the street and take a streetcar wherever I wanted to go. It was a comfortable form of transportation and there were good connections. There was a good bus system all over the city as well.

I found Helsinki to be a beautiful city almost encircled by water. It sits on the north side of the gulf and is warmed by this body of water so that in the summer it is lush and green. It's a cosmopolitan city with ultra-modern architecture, stately cathedrals, tree-lined streets, and small parks dotting the whole area.

As soon as we were settled I hurried to the Sibelius Academy, only a walking distance away, and registered for the spring semester. How excited I was to be stepping through the massive doors of the academy for the first time. I wished mother could see me there. I was going to get my wish and become a teacher of music. I was determined to achieve that goal.

Finally spring arrived. Our little park came to life. The trees were full of buds, the pond began taking on colors. Nature was waking up from its long sleep. I too was waking up from my childhood into maturity. Expecting a baby made me feel mature and responsible. I had high hopes that everything would be all right and that I would be respected by Jorma and his parents after the baby was born.

The frost had hardly melted from the ground when the blue anemone, which I adored, lifted its delicate little head through the thin crust of snow. Jorma had bought a cute little summer cottage at Lappa Lake about fifty kilometers from Helsinki where we were to spend all our weekends as soon as the snow was gone. I could hardly wait. It was a peaceful spot in the midst of a deep forest, but right by the water. Away from the noise of the city, you could hear the winds blow and the soft swish of the water on the shore.

There was a small sauna right next to the water and from the narrow wooden pier you could conveniently jump right into the water after a hot sauna bath. We could also pick fresh mushrooms in the nearby woods, or go fishing on the enchanting Lake Lappa. The most interesting thing we did was to hunt for crawfish, using our own handmade traps. This trap, a wooden hoop about two feet in diameter with a piece of netting around it, was placed in shallow water with a long sapling attached to it. With this sapling we would raise the trap to check it periodically, collecting the crawfish that had gone after our bait and fallen into the net. That was a lot of fun and sometimes we had a dozen in one trap. Then we placed them in another box with net siding and let the water run through it to clean the crawfish and left the box in shallow water so that we could periodically feed them oatmeal porridge, which they loved, and become big and fat. Sometimes we could collect as many as 200 of these delicate tidbits, and when guests arrived, Liisi cooked them in salted boiling water with a lot of fresh dill for ten to fifteen minutes and they were ready to eat. At big crawfish parties called *Rapu-kesti* folks would eat tail after tail, the tail being the best part, and follow each one with a glass of *Snapps* (a hard drink).

My child was born at the beginning of summer, just as all the beautiful migratory birds returned to Finland and the cuckoo bird announced the summer with its fascinating call. My little boy was given the name Harri, after his grandfather, and I took great delight in him, singing to him and cuddling him at every possible moment. He was a big 7.5 kilo boy at birth and got along very fine. I loved him more than anything in the world, and when I was busy with my music studies, Liisi proudly took care of him.

Harri was a good, healthy baby. He was blond and blue-

41

eyed and the image of Jorma. When he was five months old, he had his first little tooth and another followed soon after. He giggled and laughed while playing with his toes, and he listened so quietly when I played the piano. To me he was the best and cutest baby in the world, and I was very proud of him. Jorma, my thoughtful husband had bought me a small mahagony piano and I enjoyed it tremendously. He was gone a lot on business trips, but I had my baby and my piano to keep me busy.

Then one weekend in the fall he brought his secretary to our cabin. She was a friendly, Swedish-speaking woman in her thirties, of medium height with quick, piercing brown eyes. Her name was Anitra. I had met her once before; she told me then that she would like to come to our cabin, but she hated fishing because she considered it to be torturing the fish.

Anitra's visits became regular, and most of the time while I was busy with Harri, Jorma and she took long walks in the woods. They seemed to enjoy each other's company. One day, while Jorma was taking a sauna, Anitra confided in me that she had a secret love affair the previous summer in London. She proudly showed me the solid gold bracelet she had received from her lover and went on to tell me how she had met the man in a nightclub, while his wife was away with their five-year-old son, and they had fallen madly in love. Anitra had hoped that the man would marry her, but when his wife returned he told Anitra he didn't want to lose his son. That was the end of their romance. She seemed a little sad and tears came to her eyes as she showed me a picture of her love and his son. I sympathized with her but was glad the father had chosen to stay with his son.

The relationship between myself and Jorma's parents hadn't changed much. They were very dignified, aloof people. I felt they criticized every move I made. There were nine children in their family, seven boys and two girls. They were all very smart and good-looking children. I especially remember Meri, the oldest girl, who was so pretty and who had studied to be an architect. I was closest to the baby in the family, a nine-year-old, Tipsa, with whom I sang and played.

But, I was never really at home in that family and was frightened every time we were invited to dinner. It seemed to me I was always getting scolded about something or other and the that other children enjoyed having someone else be the target of criticism, I hated it and felt like the stupid fool of the family. I remember sitting at the dinner table listening to their remarks. My skirts were too short or too long, my clothes were not presentable for the wife of a prominent man. "What a pity you don't look more like a mother rather than a fifteen-year-old," I can still hear my mother-in-law saying. I would cringe every time I thought she was going to speak to me.

There was an unfortunate mishap that almost broke up our marriage. It was when Harri was about six months old and Jorma's parents had come to our cabin, which happened very seldom, to see their grandson. They stayed overnight and while everyone was asleep, early in the morning, I got up to change Harri's diapers. It was still quite dark and we had no electricity. There was only a very dimly lit oil lamp guiding my way. Everything I needed for the baby was neatly in its place on the shelf, including the bottles of medications and ointments I had received from the hospital. There was a bottle of baby oil and a bottle of lysol which looked exactly the same in the dark, with the same white handwritten labels too. Well, accidentally I grabbed the bottle of lysol instead of the oil to rub on the baby's bottom, and the minute I had done it Harri shrieked out in pain. Although I washed him off immediately and put on some ointment, the damage was done. The poor baby kept on crying and everyone in the house

43

woke up. I was bitterly accused of stupidity and carelessness by Jorma's parents and being as terrified as I was, I could not listen to it, but ran out of the house crying hysterically. The doctor soon came and examined the baby, calming everybody down with the report that no serious damage had been done. But I sat all day and night beside Harri and shed some bitter tears. For that incident my in-laws never forgave me.

Sibelius Academy gave a spring concert in May and chose the best student performers for its program. I was fortunate to be one of them and how proud and happy I was. I would have a chance to sing in the elegant concert hall on this important occasion. I was so full of joy and confidence, and from the applause I received from the audience, I gained more hope and encouragement about my future in music. If only my mother could have been there to share in the thrills and happiness. From then on I was busier than ever with my studies.

Harri was a busy little scamp, getting into everything. He took his first steps soon after his first birthday and he seemed to develop so fast after that. Now we had great fun playing together in our little park across the street, where swans swam elegantly around the pond and rushed to get the crumbs we threw to them. Life seemed calm and pleasant then, and I was very happy with my baby. As for my music, things couldn't have been better for I had passed all the examinations the academy required.

Occasionally I felt a troubling sense of guilt because I didn't love Jorma with the ardor and passion I sometimes saw in his eyes, but I felt secure and comfortable with him. I didn't mind the demands he made on my body, but he often left me restless and with unsatisfied stirrings. However, I didn't know there could be any difference.

I hadn't seen my sister Enni for some time. She had graduated from Ebenaeser College and was soon teaching in

Kuopio, northern Finland. But sister Lea showed up one day, knocking at my door. How surprised and pleased I was to see her. She told me she had been released from the sanitorium, where I had visited her many times, and she wanted to see me and talk to me. Lea didn't look well to me but I didn't ask too many questions. I was just glad to see her, and invited her to tay for a few days, which she did. During her visit, however, I noticed that she was very restless and walked around a great deal of the time. It was a nervous kind of walking, almost as if she were pacing.

Harri was then in a nursery school and I took Lea to visit the school and to see all the children at play. I thought she would enjoy them. Jorma was away on business and, after Lea and I came home, we sat down and had a long talk. She seemed very lonesome and pessimistic, and she had no friends. "You are so popular, clever, and attractive," she said to me, "and you have been successful in your life, I have nothing." She said she always remembered my smile, and thought I had so much to smile about. "But I can't smile because I am a failure." she sobbed and I tried to console her. After we had talked for hours, I thought she felt better. We talked about everything, even about stepfather, and she admitted that she didn't want to see him anymore. She seemed happier.

It was time to retire and I put Harri in bed and crossed his little hands to say our little Finnish prayer: *"Levolle lasken Luojani. . . ."* Then I said good night to Lea, who was lying on top of her bed. I stayed up to wait for Jorma and played some soft music on the piano.

Suddenly I heard someone in the kitchen opening cupboards. Liisi had had the day off, so it couldn't be her. I decided to see if Lea needed something. She was not in the kitchen or in her room, so I peeked into Harri's room and saw something that horrified me. Lea was standing beside his bed with a large butcher knife in her hand, ready to stab him.

I ran to her quickly and grabbed the knife just in time. She was in a trance, it seemed. She looked at me but didn't seem to see me. I heard her murmur, "He would be better off dead than alive in this sinful world."

Before I had fully recovered from my shock, Lea had disappeared. Harri had been awakened by the commotion and I knelt down beside him as he opened his innocent eyes and looked at me. I grabbed him to me and couldn't stop the tears. I could not have lived without my baby, I thought.

I couldn't leave Harri alone so I waited until Jorma returned. As soon as he came in, I ran out looking for Lea but I found no trace of her. After hours of desperate waiting and worrying there was a phone call from the police station. Lea had been found wandering aimlessly on the street. After this episode we had Lea committed to a mental hospital in Helsinki.

Upon returning home from a business trip to England, Jorma showed me two presents he had purchased in London. They were two beautiful silver filigree bracelets. He asked me to choose one of them. The other one was for Anitra, he said. That shook me a little, as I remembered the story she had told me of her secret lover in London and the bracelet she had received. My eyes probably betrayed my feelings because Jorma immediately explained that all the bosses brought presents for their secretaries. So that took care of that. Nevertheless it left a little spark of doubt in my mind.

On our balcony two pigeons had made their nest and enjoyed watching and studying them. It didn't take long for Harri to also begin looking for them, watching their hustle and bustle. He was now two years old, a chubby little rascal and had started learning some words. We fed the birds seed, and I gave them a big dish full of water in which they bathed and played, turning round and round as if to show off their tricks.

46

One day I received a phone call from Lea's hospital asking me to come and visit her. It would do her some good they felt. That was one unforgettable experience that I'll never be able to erase from my mind.

Lea was in a private room and as I entered I couldn't see her anywhere. Fearfully I sat down for a moment, and then heard some commotion coming from underneath her bed. Looking closer I recognized her lying there without a stitch of clothing on. When she heard me calling her name, she slowly crawled up onto her knees and came toward me. Her hands were ice cold, her face pale and thin, and her eyes were staring at me. She didn't know me, it seemed, and her hand started listlessly touching me all over. I tried to talk to her but she didn't understand me and just mumbled something like a child would. She continued to touch my face, my eyes, and my mouth. Perhaps it felt good to her to have a human being nearby. I sat there for a long while and finally coaxed her to go to bed and then covered her up with a blanket. Then I rang for the nurse, and we left the room.

From the room next door some animal-like grunting could be heard. Sometime it was laughing, sometimes screaming and yelling. I shivered. The nurse told me the room was an isolation cell with padded walls and no windows, and no furniture other than one chair which the patient was tied to. As we walked through a long hall where more stable patients were moving about, one man ran to me, took hold of my arm and cried: "Don't go away, please don't go," and he grinned so pitifully at me.

At home again, I felt sick and exhausted. The experience had been too much. For a long time I sat and tried to comprehend the incident. I truly felt at that moment that a human being is nothing but a bird in flight, up against a furious wind. Some are lucky and find a place to light and take shelter, others never do and just keep on struggling against terrible odds.

The time went on. Harri was now four years old and I was on my last semester at the Academy. How happy I was to know that I had almost accomplished what Mother and I had planned for me, a musical career. I was especially proud to have had a chance to study the music of our genius composer, Jean Sibelius, and to be able to analyze his great works. Often while listening to his fifth symphony I could hear the birds sing, the howling of the storm, and I felt my Finland. It is in his symphonies that his greatness is revealed. They are full of the refreshing gaiety of the snow and ice and laughter. He also composed such popular pieces as "Valse Triste" and a group of songs with which I grew very familiar. Sibelius had been considered to be an important figure in the worthy procession of composers all around the world.

CHAPTER 8
Bitter Tears

One sunny Monday afternoon, just before my graduation, I was walking in Kaivopuisto Park with Harri, near the home of Jorma's parents, when I noticed two people walking slowly hand in hand in front of me. I immediately recognized them as Jorma and Anitra. Oh, God. My heart stopped. What were they doing here? I didn't usually come to this park, but this time I had gone to my in-laws' house to get Harri who had been visiting them while I took one of my final examinations. I stopped in my tracks, but Harri had already recognized his father and called him. Jorma turned around, saw us, dropped Anitra's hand and came closer, "Hi, we just had lunch over there," he said, and pointed to a restaurant nearby. Both of them looked very embarrassed and uncomfortable. I couldn't say a word, just turned around, took Harri by the hand and walked away. They continued their walk and disappeared. I thought of the bracelet Jorma had given Anitra, her story about her lover in London, and the walks in the woods Jorma and Anitra had taken in Lappa Lake. Of course, it was so obvious now. Why hadn't I seen it before?

That night I laid in bed fully awake and stared at the ceiling. I felt pushed aside, confused and bitter. I don't belong to anyone. Nobody wants or needs my love. I cried.

There were times in our marriage when Jorma and I had walked in different rhythms, but this was different. This was serious. After that episode, life went on as usual. Jorma didn't touch the subject, nor did I. But he never physically contacted me.

One day, late in May, I got an unexpected visitor, Anitra. She told me right out that Jorma and she were in love and they were going to get married as soon as possible. She accused me of being too young and immature, too inexperienced in sexual life to be able to hold a man. Also she pointed out, that the cabin at Lappa Lake was Jorma's, not mine. I should pack and leave. What a terrible message! I stared at her in shock and disbelief. She seemed so determined to win the battle and it left me speechless. What had I done to deserve this? What was I going to do? I was completely helpless, a twenty-one-year-old girl, alone with a big problem. There was no one to turn to, to get advice from. Stepfather, I knew, was out of the question. My sisters were far away. I had no relative or close friend I could have confided in. Thank God I was just about finished with my studies and hopefully could get a job to support Harri and myself. All I really wanted now was my child, my love and joy. My head was swimming, I felt dizzy. All my life I had been told what to do or what not to do. Now I stood alone. I felt lost, homeless!

Jorma moved out of the house and sent his brother John, a lawyer, to talk to me. The divorce action took place at the

Municipal Court in Helsinki. I was given the custody of our child and Jorma was ordered to pay me alimony, which barely met our needs.

Sibelius Academy was about to graduate the class of 1939. It was a happy crowd which flowed out of the Conservatory's mighty doors now on the threshold of a new life. I was one of them. After four years of preparation I was finally on my way, having reached my goal, a teacher of music. Oh, how I wished my Mother could share the joy and pride.

Sometimes I sat alone, still stunned, wondering what to do. I would miss Jorma, the first man in my life. I didn't blame him for leaving me, but I blamed Anitra for stealing him from me and our son. In my sadness I turned to my music and played my piano for hours. Little by little the numbness began to leave me. It was so good to know I had my child to live for, come what may.

Harri was a happy fellow. He was handsome, intelligent, and independent. We had fun building pyramids out of blocks, coloring and drawing, and, of course, playing the piano and singing. He enjoyed music and could carry a tune well. I planned to start teaching him piano very soon.

To help with our finances, I rented our guest room to a student friend of mine. She paid for room and board. Liisi, who still wanted to stay with us, took care of her as well as the rest of us. My friend Elsi was in her last year of school at the Academy, majoring in piano. When the spring semester was over, she took private piano lessons and worked part-time. She was good company for me and in her free time we played piano and sang duets together. Tall and thin Elsie, with her large brown eyes and bleached blond hair, was so good-natured and kind. I'll never forget when she walked down the street, how her upper torso swayed from side to side reminding me of a sailboat in the wind.

When summer arrived, the people of Helsinki packed up and took off for their annual stay in the country, at a summer cottage by a lake or in a cabin on an island. Everyone who was able, got away to enjoy the sunlight and warmth, which is so brief in the Finnish summer. This year, however, Harri and I had to stay in the city, so we took trips by bus to the sandy beaches.

One Sunday afternoon in the middle of summer Harri and I boarded a bus to the beach. He enjoyed those trips so much and pointed out everything he saw through the windows of the bus. Nature was alive with color and the blue sky had piles of big cumulous clouds, and the sunlight was glaringly bright. Harri couldn't get enough of playing and splashing in the water and on the sandy beach. His laughter echoed above all the noises and I loved to hear it. That was a happy sound, and it had been a happy day.

The following day I had an appointment with the school director at Jarvenpaa Junior College, where I had applied for a position as a music teacher beginning in the fall. Liisi took care of Harri while I was gone. Everything went well and I had my assurance of the position in my pocket, and returned home joyful and full of good news. But my Harri was gone. Liisi's tearful face at the door told me something was wrong. Between sobs, she told me that my mother-in-law had come to get Harri and was very demanding. I asked her when she was going to bring Harri back, Liisi told me: "She said never! and shut the door."

If you are one of those unfortunate people who have lost a child you know how it feels. I was stunned and what I felt I couldn't express. I picked up the telephone immediately and called the home of my in-laws. There was no answer. In my worry and desperation I decided to call stepfather at his home on the West Coast. He was my last hope. Certainly he would know what to do to get Harri back. I would beg him to help me, for the child had been granted to me in court. He was mine!

But I was wrong. When stepfather came to the phone

and I asked him for advice he explained: "I am not your father! You are now involved with my blood relatives and you will have to settle your own problems. Yet there is one thing I will tell you now. You cannot, must not, fight for the ownership of your son. You have nothing to offer to him, no wealth, no name. Your in-laws have everything. They are highly esteemed people and can give Harri a future, you can't. You must not be selfish, Vikki, and drag him down to your level in these circumstances. Remember this, you have nothing and you are nothing!"

"But what about my love for Harri?" I cried. "Isn't it worth something?" But stepfather hadn't heard me. He was gone and the receiver clicked in my ear.

I was hit hard. His words cut through me like a knife. Again I had been told that I was nothing, immature, irresponsible. I wanted to cry out but nothing came out. I felt torn to pieces. What was wrong with me? Had I really not accomplished anything? I cried so much that night that I thought there would be no more tears left in me. I felt only half alive.

That night is still with me. It is like yesterday's horrible nightmare. Not until then did I dare rebel against my stepfather, but from that time on I felt nothing but resentment and bitterness against stepfather's domination. He had abandoned me!

The following morning I was able to make an important decision. I was not going to lose my mind as sister Lea had. I would have to grow, be strong, and show everyone that I was worth something, and could get what I wanted. "I may have no right to get him now," I thought to myself, "but there will come a day when I'll get him back."

The summer was at its peak. As I opened the door to the balcony a cool breeze had come up from the East, taking the edge off the intense afternoon heat. The breeze felt good on my burning temples, and the wind relaxed my body. I arranged some flowers in a vase. They were the light blue forget-me-nots which Harri had picked for me on our beach trip—they were so fragile, so poised, and so still, and they made me think of my mother. Just like the flowers in the vase in front of me, I had always put my mother on a pedestal. She was for me a flawless example of a human being, the kind I wanted to be some day. I remembered how cheery she had always looked, especially after arriving home from her trip to Europe. Thinking of her kindled a new spark in my mind, a new hope that maybe I too could find some happiness somewhere in the big, wide world. I decided to find out about the possibilities.

I went to my piano and played "our song" over and over again and as if Mother had been standing by me, I felt better, stronger. I had to make things work for the sake of my child and for myself as well, and for my mother. I thought of Harri for a long time thereafter. I woke up thinking of him, I went to bed thinking of him. And I felt, I will grow strong for him!

But why didn't I fight back? Why didn't I stick to my rights? Because I was a coward—afraid of punishment. Because I had always been forced to obey those who were ruling my life.

CHAPTER 9
Rolph

I needed time to make myself feel like a whole person again and to trust in my own abilities. But it wasn't easy for me, especially alone as I was. Yet I didn't want to have anything to do with a man, any man. I was hurt and wanted to be left alone.

After all the traumatic experiences, my body seemed to be protesting. I didn't feel good so much of the time. Therefore, I decided to get involved in an activity. I took up tennis and joined the Helsinki Tennis Club. Elsie was a member there and together we now started to practice several times a week. I had a good background, having played with step-father and my teacher, Mr. Martinson, years before.

I didn't take long before I won the class B tournament, received a trophy and was automatically put into class A. That meant I was chosen to play singles, doubles, and mixed matches in tournaments with other clubs. Elsie and I played together a lot and she too was soon able to get into class A. In the summer we played outdoors, in the winter on the club's own indoor court.

Practicing for tournaments. Elsie and I also doubled with other women, and for mixed games, with different men. There were a couple of young men that we were requested to practice with, a pair of Germans now studying at Helsinki Poly, Wolde and Rolph. They were intelligent, handsome, and pleasant. Both were born in St. Petersburg, Russia during the revolution, and their parents, like so many others at that time, had fled to Estonia and settled in Tallinna, the capital. Both fellows spoke fluent Finnish and Swedish, as well as many other languages.

We were a good mixed tennis team and played together in many tournaments. Elsie soon fell in love with Wolde, the blond and blue-eyed one, and they started going out evenings. Rolph tried to approach me with his charming personality and good looks. He was very tall and slender, with broad shoulders and a slim waist. His eyes were lustrous brown and his hair a deep, dark brown. But no man interested me. I talked to him and listened to his stories about his family, and the classical music he was so interested in, but I didn't want to be involved any more than that. I remained unapproachable to all of his advances and continued to make my way alone.

Our tennis matches continued and we sometimes traveled long distances. Tournaments sometimes took us out of the country, and I enjoyed the change of scenery. It did me good to get my thoughts off my child and our tragedy. I would be starting my teaching job at Jarvenpaa Junior Collge later in the fall and I looked forward to that very much. I could hardly wait to get involved in my work.

September is the month when the migratory birds leave Finland, and as we say in Finland, the Cuckoo Bird loses its voice in the fall, because it doesn't sing anymore. Our club had a tournament that month in Tallinna, Estonia where Rolph's parents lived. He had arranged it so that all four of us could spend the night in his parents' home.

The trip was delightful on our luxury liner from Helsinki to Tallinna. We played well that day and won our mixed match 6-2 and 6-4. Rolph was a brilliant tennis player. After the tournament we all drove to his parents' home on Beach Street. I entered the house with very mixed feelings. I had had such bad experiences with "parents" that I froze when introduced to Rolph's mother and father. To my big surprise, however, we were met with such overwhelming warmth and politeness that I immediately felt at home. His parents used the German language when conversing with us but the Russian language with Rolph.

Rolph's father, called Grauchen, was a big-bellied, white-haired gentleman, kind and gentle, with a sweet shyness about him. He was an engineer. His wife was small and thin, with gray hair piled neatly on top of her head and with those lustrous brown eyes I had seen on Rolph. He was the image of his mother.

We had an excellent dinner at their home. There was Russian borsch and meat rulladen, which their maid Anna had prepared. And later, to top it all off there was champagne for our tennis victory. Then we all sat and listened to a beautiful concert performed by Rolph's Uncle Walter, who had come for a visit. He was the organist in the huge St. Peter's Church in Tallinna. He played on and on—Bach, Beethoven, Tchaikovski—and I listened with my eyes closed, imagining my mother there playing. Since her death I had heard no one play like that, so sincere, so full of emotion. I felt that those memorable moments are so few and so rare. They are moments of perfection to me and they make time stand still.

After that trip I had the desire to go to mother's grave, to be alone with my thoughts, and to feel her presence. That chapel was always a sanctuary for me since her burial. I bought a bouquet of flowers, the porcelain-like lavender sweet peas, which I placed in the vase next to her name plate and as I knelt in front of her grave I felt she was with me.

One evening Elsie invited Wolde and Rolph for dinner at our apartment. Liisi had made a typical Finnish dish called *Kalakukko* (fish pie). The bread is out of rye flour and the filling is a small fish called *Muikku*. One eats bones and all since it is cooked for four to six hours until the bones are soft. Both men loved it and praised Liisi.

After dinner Elsie and I played duets on the piano and then Wolde asked Rolph to sing. I offered to accompany him and he sang the beautiful and well-known "Autumn Leaves." His voice was very dark but soft and he sang with a lot of feeling. I was surprised and liked it very much and found myself humming the song long after our guests were gone. But I didn't want to be involved with any man, I thought. Funny that it even came to my mind.

Before going to bed that night I stopped in front of the window. The sun had gone down long ago but the pale moon rose red from behind the edge of the woods and it brightened the area with its pale light and made strange shadows of the birch trees in the park. I stood there for a long time and thought of my past. I had never known one could feel so lonesome, especially on a night like this. I made a promise to myself then: I would only look forward, never back, and try to make the best of my life.

It was about that time that the war broke out in Europe. The Germans had invaded Poland. We in the north thought we could stay out of it and, meanwhile, we waited and anxiously watched its development. The big question for Finland was, what will Russia do?

That fall we played tennis in Turku, traveling there by train. I was happy about going and my feet felt as if they were dancing down the streets. I wasn't sure of the reason until I sat on the train next to Rolph and his hand touched mine. I pulled it back as soon a I could. Then I decided it hadn't been all that unpleasant and I almost wished that I'd left it there a moment longer. I found myself longing to be touched by someone. But I couldn't admit it to myself, not yet. A voice inside of me was saying, "Vikki, you don't want another man, ever!" Yet, I wasn't so sure about it anymore.

The tournament went fine and we returned home the next day. When Rolph said goodbye to me at my door he said, "Let me help you to overcome your fear, Vikki. I don't ask for anything more." I answered with relief, "Thank you, Rolph." I felt exhausted and troubled. I liked his company, but that had to be all. I wanted to remain inaccessible to all his advances.

Once when Rolph must have felt particularly frustrated over my treatment of him he asked me, "What am I doing wrong, Vikki, that you always push me away?"

"It isn't you," I replied. "I like you, Rolph, but there has been something in my past that prevents me from opening up to you. I don't want to be hurt by anyone, ever again."

Then I went on to explain that I wanted to grow and to prove myself, to prove that I was a worthwhile person, and before I could do that, I had to be alone. He looked at me with those charming dark eyes full of understanding, but said nothing. I knew I liked him then, more than I wanted to.

We became more friendly toward each other after that, and I noticed that I missed him if he didn't come to play tennis sometimes. The idea that he might have a girlfriend hadn't bothered me the slightest before, but now it started entering my mind and making me uneasy. Rolph knew he was a good-looking man. Every time he walked down the street, girls would look at him. He liked to dress well and I remember him in his gray, snugly fitting long coat, black hat, white gloves and shiney black cane. I didn't want to admit it, but I was beginning to feel some jealousy.

One day in the late afternon I took the bus to the beach where Harri and I used to go. I hadn't seen Rolph for several days and was feeling depressed, so I thought it would do me some good. The sun sank slowly into the sea as I entered the park, and the surface of the water looked like blood. The beach was shadowed and empty.

A strong feeling came upon me. I wanted to see my son in the same spot where I had seen him on that last day. I wanted to hear his laughter, to see him jumping in the water so happily, like before. But he wasn't there. He had been taken away to Lohja, far from Helsinki, where his father and Anitra now lived. I could only hope that one day soon I would be seeing him again and holding him in my arms. Oh, Mother, if you could see me now. The laughter is gone from my face and I cannot sing our song!

The following day Rolph called me. He had been home in Estonia to see his parents and he told me that the war situation in central Europe was becoming more and more critical. It was beginning to spread out and the small countries by the Baltic—Estonia, Latvia, and Lithuania—were shivering in fright. Rolph was very worried about his elderly parents, who had already fled from Russia during the revolution in 1917. If the war situation got worse, he pointed out, he would have to leave Finland and go to rescue his parents.

I was happy to hear from Rolph, but sad to think of him leaving the country. He asked me to have dinner with him that night and I accepted. I decided I would wear my blue dress, the one with the white collar and buttons down the front. It matched the color of my eyes. I wanted to look pretty.

We had dinner at Kamp's Restaurant with champagne and broiled lobster, but I saw only him. I felt a sudden surge of affection for him and I touched his arm softly. I knew then that I had found someone who was everything I had dreamed of. My bitterness was gone.

After dinner we walked hand in hand down the colorful Esplanade and sat on a bench listening to soft music coming from the Kappeli Restaurant nearby. Then we walked down the beautiful tree-lined promenade, stopping by a large oak tree. He leaned against its brown trunk and started to sing: "*Kukkivat tuomien valkoiset tertut. . . .* " It was the bird-cherry tree lovesong. I moved toward him and looked lovingly into his eyes. We kissed. How beautiful and good life was then.

Our romance had begun, and I danced down the streets of Helsinki in a fever. I saw Rolph's lustrous eyes everywhere and I could smell the exciting English Leather on his freshly shaven face and feel his strong arms caress me. It was wonderful to be in love for the first time in my life. These feelings were new to me and the power of them was so great it was as if my heart were breaking. I needed love desperately. Now followed the most wonderful days and weeks, rendezvous, music, dancing, walks in the park, and all the time growing more in love.

Then there was the night in September I shall never forget. It happened in Kaivopuisto Park. We walked hand in hand to the waterfront where the waves were gently nudging the shore, and sat on a mat of fallen leaves. It felt so soft and fluffy beneath us. Rolph reached into his pocket, pulled out a small box, opened it and handed me a diamond ring, a ring more gorgeous than I had ever seen before. He had tears in his eyes when he put it on my finger and whispered in my ear: "Darling, I love you, and I want you to be mine forever." He was so tender and affectionate, and he pulled me to him and kissed me passionately. I pressed myself against his chest and we were lost in each other's arms. Yes, Rolph was my prince, my idol! The love we shared was our bond, our hold on life and we wanted to make the best of it. A few days later Rolph received a desperate message from his parents telling him that Estonia, Latvia, and Lithuania had fallen under Soviet power and that large groups of people had already left their homeland by boat. There had been newspaper reports in circulation in Finland for several weeks keeping people posted on the events of the war, but this was the most tragic news yet. The Estonian government was urging its citizens to flee if they could. It was a shock to both of us. What should we do?

The message continued: "We are ready to leave for Germany at the first opportunity. Follow us as soon as you can and look for us in Stettin at Uncle Hugo's. No use trying to come to Estonia. It is already in turmoil. You couldn't survive." Russia was ready to pounce.

That same day the Finnish newspapers were reporting the fate of the Baltic countries and announced that Russia was pressuring our homeland as well. The Finnish government considered this a sign that we were next to fall. Delegates were sent to Moscow for negotiations. The Soviets were requiring that the Finns allow a few of their islands to be fortified.

In anticipation of events such as this the Finnish government had already begun fortifications on the eastern border. We were expecting a possible invasion, and it did come at the end of November.

The people of Finland were getting ready. Many student volunteers, young collge boys, were helping to build lines of fortification in Kannas, near the Russian border. Most of the colleges, including my future teaching place, were not going to open for the fall semester. Air raid shelters were being built, and there was a good deal of blackout practice. First aid stations were established, fire fighters were trained. The Lotta Svard and the Red Cross were calling for volunteers.

Talk of war on the radio and in the press increased. We were told to paste strips of paper on the windows to protect them from breakage during air raids. Bath tubs were always to be filled with water in case of fires and every house was to have sandbags at hand. I had not taken any precautions for the simple reason that I, like many others, did not believe there would be a war. I was sure it was only a threat.

The negotiations between Russia and Finland ended in failure and Russian troops opened fire in late November 1939. The fright and shock over the fate of my country left me in a state of bewilderment. I didn't sleep well but walked the floor trying to make up my mind whether to leave my beloved country and go with my fiance to an unknown destination or to stay here. When Rolph came early the next morning to see me, I had made up my mind.

"Why haven't you started packing yet, darling?" Rolph asked me, as he entered my apartment. I took one look at him. He looked so handsome and charming. It was extremely difficult for me to tell him that I wasn't going to go with him.

"Rolph, dearest, I stayed awake all night trying to make up my mind about our future. The easiest for me would be to leave my country, follow you, and let you take the burden of caring for both of us. But you are strong and determined and I know you can get through this without me. My country needs every man and woman. I feel an obligation to Finland and my people. And there is my son, whom I am determined to get back some day. It wouldn't be right to leave now!"

Rolph stared at me, speechless and uncomprehending. He spoke, with sadness showing in his face.

"But I don't belong here. I don't belong anywhere. I was

born in Russia, grew up in Estonia, and now have nowhere to go." He pointed out that all of his uncles and aunts were now in Germany, and it was beckoning to him. Germany was strong, it welcomed all refugees, its schools were open and there was food and clothing for everyone.

"I need to belong somewhere and get a new start. And a wife should go with her husband," he added.

I was startled for a minute and had to gather strength to go on.

"I will never forgive myself if I run away from my responsibilities here. I just can't leave now!"

Rolph turned around and, without looking at me, walked to the door and left my apartment. As soon as he was gone I broke down in bitter tears.

My love, my future dreams, were shattered.

CHAPTER 10
The First Bombing of Helsinki

It was November 30, 1939, about seven A.M. The morning sun shone brightly in the clear autumn sky. I had just looked out my window to watch the traffic on the street below, when my attention was suddenly drawn to the people staring up at the sky. Then they began to run helplessly this way and that. Panic had set in. Just then sirens started screaming, and people echoed them back. I was nailed to the floor as I stared out at the crowds of frantic people.

At that moment six Russian airplanes flew toward the center of the city. These were followed by three more. I saw them sparkling in the sunshine like silver birds. Anti-aircraft fire could be heard in the distance and small puffs of smoke appeared around the planes. Machine guns rattled. The fear of death crept over me. Bombs!

A terrible roar shook the whole city followed by a deathly stillness which lasted but a second. Then screams, panic, and chaos outside. I was still nailed to the floor and couldn't move. Through the window I could see black pillars of smoke rising from the burning buildings.

This was war. There was no doubt about it anymore. I trembled, and with shaking hands I started to dress as quickly as I could. I heard sounds of running feet and the cries of women and children. My knees shook. I grabbed what I thought were valuables I couldn't leave behind and packed them. In my panic I grabbed so many useless and unnecessary items.

My load was heavy and my knees almost buckled as I descended into the basement where the other occupants of the building were already gathered. Some were standing, some sitting, all waiting for further developments. On every face the gravity of the situation was plainly visible. Here and there I could see mothers clinging to their children. I was reminded of my own son. Would the war reach the small town of Lohja where he now lived? And where was Rolph? My heart pounded and I had a strong urge to go to him. I had to find out if he was all right. Oh, God, what was in store for all of us?

The enemy renewed the attack after a few hours. I had been on my way to search for Rolph on Lonnroth Street. He might have gone to his college there, I thought. I stopped in my tracks. Again there was that ear-splitting scream of the sirens, then the steady roar of the bombers as they approached. I counted one, two, three, as they circled over Toolo Bay, speeding towards the east. Then they separated and prepared for attack. There was that frightful whining and whistling in the air, then the bombs rained down. I was thrown against a parked truck and someone pulled me under it. The day had turned to night in the blinding smoke. I closed my eyes and prayed.

Heavy smoke still hung over him as he regained consciousness. Aside from the discomfort of compression in his lungs, Rolph was intact, lying on Lonnroth street. He had been on his way to the Institute of Technology. He crawled slowly from the debris and rubble and sat on the curb. His aching head cleared slightly as the acid smoke disappeared. An ambulance screamed its way through the debris-filled streets. There was a blur of activity before him, stretchers, white-coated attendants, and he was whisked away. He blacked out again.

All around me was a great din and the earth shook under me. Building after building was crumbling. There were sparks hissing and shooting all around. Rolph's school was in ruins. My temples were pounding and I was choking. I crawled out from under the truck. My arm ached from a blow it had received in the blast. I checked. I could move it. It wasn't broken. Stumbling over the rubble here and there, I hurried home.

By evening there was a steady stream of people fleeing. Passing by our building, moving down the street in droves were people on foot. Others, more fortunate, rode. Everyone carried parcels of belongings as big as they could possibly manage. Many of them had no certain destination but were simply going into the nearby woods and small towns.

An unexpected knock on my door brought me to my senses. Opening the door I almost fainted with relief. My beloved fiancé stood there—haggard, bruised, but alive. I clung to him desperately. We were together again, and we kissed and kissed.

Rolph told me that he had contacted the German Consulate in Helsinki and was told that there were no ships leaving for Germany or anywhere. The waters were all mined. Furthermore, there was a new order that barred anyone from leaving the country. I thanked God for that turn of events.

Now he was mine to have, to hold. I loved him and adored him. He was my big and strong dark-eyed man and I leaned on him, soaking in his warmth and his tender touch. He was so exciting and affectionate, so different from Jorma, and I longed for joining my body to his. A surge of joy passed through me as he held me in his embrace, and kissed me. But this wasn't just a kiss, it was a lifetime promise.

CHAPTER 11
Luck Was with Me

One evening our janitor went around counting the tenants that remained. It was his duty to turn off the hot water and to regulate the heat. He found only six persons left in the eight-story building. I was one of them. My friend Elsie had married Wolde and had moved away from Helsinki. Liisi had gone home, since I didn't need her anymore. I was alone again.

We, the six remaining people, now formed a mutual assistance pact in which each one promised to carry out certain duties in the case of an emergency. My job was to give first aid to casualties. I had taken a course in first aid given by the Finnish Red Cross. Nearly every woman in Helsinki had taken these courses. A small kit containing bandages and supplies was always within reach.

An opportunity to offer my services came soon. An elderly woman who had broken her leg while hurrying into our cellar during a raid needed aid. I was able to support her leg with a splint and a tight wrapping. She was later taken to a hospital for further treatment.

The janitor's wife, a thin, shriveled up woman of middle age, made coffee for everybody who came to our shelter, and despite the fact that the coffee was nothing but synthetic, it meant a great deal to us. It helped to get us through those long waiting periods when raids would last for several hours.

The temperature in our rooms became lower and lower until we were forced to put on all our outdoor garments to keep warm. Many people didn't dare to undress at all for fear they would not be able to dress quickly enough in the event of a raid. Some even dragged their bedding into the shelters and slept there all of the time, raid or no raid.

The air raid shelters were not always adequate but in most cases they offered considerable protection. Our basement had been reinforced by upright beams, and windows were reinforced with sandbags, inside and out. We had benches and platforms for people to make themselves comfortable and a stretcher for emergency use.

As we became accustomed to the long stays in the shelter we devised interesting means of passing the time. We sang folk songs or read books or played games. The women knitted socks and garments for soldiers at the front.

Gradually people all over the city began to volunteer their services to aid in the war effort. Rolph offered his services to a defense program, and I registered at the hospital on Lonnroth Street with other young women students. Day and night we made bandages. Salves and medicines were also made, under the supervision of pharmacists and doctors. All products were packaged and sent to the war front. We were given a meal of soup in the hospital field kitchen and we all tried to get as much done as possible. Only when I found myself falling asleep standing up did I feel I could go home and rest for a few hours.

Eventually this hospital became a target for bombs, as had so many others, and I went to look for other work. One cold, cold day in midwinter I was assigned to accompany an elderly woman, who was an invalid, out to the country by auto. Rolph volunteered to drive the car. We were driving along a snowy, icy road. On each side you could see tracks of the war. The grenades had left their traces everywhere. There was so much lying in ruin, trees with their tops lopped off, trees lying on their sides, cars flung crosswise in the road or sitting in ditches, buildings with their sides gouged out and their interiors exposed or blasted to pieces. We felt lucky to reach our destination without mishap.

Our return trip was different. We were just nearing Helsinki when we saw planes flying above and behind us. A hasty glance showed us that a Russian plane was flying very low along our road and strafing the road. Seeing that we could not get away from its line of fire Rolph drove the car straight into the ditch. The plane whizzed past and bullets flew all around, several of them piercing the top of our car. Our guardian angel must have been with us, for we escaped injury. We crawled out from the car and walked the rest of the way into the city, unnerved and shaking quite a bit.

At the outskirts of the city we saw a crowd of people gathered around an object on the ground. Upon closer inspection we saw that it was the plane that had tried to shorten our lives. It had been shot down, and word had it that it had been piloted by a woman. Her body had already been removed, but among the wreckage a mongrel dog licked a pool of blood which was the only evidence of where she had lain.

When the war had started there were adequate supplies of food, but not long after panic buying set in and those who could afford it bought large quantities, leaving little or nothing for the rest of us. The food situation quickly became critical. Rationing was established but by then many items had become unavailable. We had to be satisfied with many substitutes. Coffee, tea, cocoa, and spices were sold out and sugar could only be secured in very small portions with a ration card. Tobacco and alcoholic beverages were scarce and extremely high in price.

Fuel shortages became evident during the long and extremely cold winter of 1939–40. Hot water was a thing of the past and houses were barely heated at all. Those who still had wood burning stoves went to the nearby woods and gathered branches and cones to keep warm, but only a very few in the city found it possible to do so since gas and elecric stoves had long since come in to replace the "old fashioned" wood burner. Most people just dressed as warmly as possible wearing ski pants and boots day in and day out.

In spite of the fact that all schools and colleges were closed, young people continued to stream into the city. It was probably the lure of new excitement that drew them there. Some, of course, wanted to help in defense work but many more came to look on. Many of those could have saved their lives if they had stayed out of Helsinki.

The time came when the children and aged were ordered evacuated from the city. A great many people had already left, that is, all who had somewhere to go. Perhaps I, too, in my first terror might have rushed away to be with my family, if I had had any. Since my stepfather remarried, I had no home.

The enemy planes flew in all directions over our country and hurled their destructive bombs everywhere on top of our cities and towns. The frost was almost unbearable that year, registering sometimes down to minus 50° Celsius, and all our thousands of lakes were frozen solid, enabling the Soviets to cross with their massive tanks wherever they desired.

They had millions of soldiers in arms and my country consisted only of about four million people. Again and again new waves of fresh enemy troops attacked our small groups of brave men. We stood alone. The whole world felt for us, thinking that our huge enemy would swallow us completely in no time. Even America, in whom we had hoped for help, gave us only sympathy.

Rolph spent most of his time up on the roof. He was now part of the Anti-aircraft Service, and I saw very little of him. But I was very proud of him for taking part in the defense of my country.

In the meantime I was hired to work in an underground arms factory helping to feed the 150 workers there. Later I worked as a cashier in the factory office. Part of this outfit was soon moved to Kapyla and I was transferred with it.

Every morning I had to catch the first streetcar going that way at six A.M., and it took over an hour to make the trip. From the last station I had a half-hour's walk along the road where a great many anti-aircraft guns were concentrating their fire. It was during one of these walks home one day that I faced enemy gunfire.

I was rushing down the road because I heard the siren signaling an air raid. All of a sudden there was a terrific blast from the guns that tumbled me into a snowbank, and as I lay there I saw tongues of flames flashing through the air. What a blast. After recovering from the impact and my state of shock I made for the trees and not any too soon. Shell fragments were hitting everything in sight.

But luck was with me, once again. I escaped without injury.

CHAPTER 12
Estonia Falls

We heard dire rumors about the fate of our neighboring country, Estonia. Now and then there would be a trickle of refugees arriving in Helsinki, telling of hard fighting in different parts of that country. We had heard nothing from Rolph's parents since their last message before leaving for Germany. Many people had fled, and we wondered how many were left to face the Russian advance. Estonia couldn't possibly defend itself against such a powerful opponent, we thought, especially when so many had fled.

A great many young men were taken prisoner in Estonia and sent to Siberia, we learned. Rumors of torture and forced labor grew day by day. One of the stories of horror that reached us concerned the wives of the Estonian military officers. The Russians forced them to march naked in the public square until they dropped. Then they were forced to make their own hangman's noose and they were hung before the horrified stares of the helpless citizens.

Rolph was anxious about his parents. One evening, just as I returned from Käpylä, I found Rolph waiting for me at my door. I had missed him so much and I was joyous at seeing him there. We had so much to talk about. Rolph had news of his parents, and I couldn't wait to hear it. We sat down immediately so he could fill me in.

An old classmate of Rolph's had escaped from Estonia before the Russian entry and had come to see him with a message from his parents. The friend, Hans, had helped Rolph's parents get on a small freighter to Luebeck, Germany. He had left them at the freighter, and as far as he knew, they were alive and out of Estonia. They indicated that they would stop in Stettin, Germany, and leave a note for Rolph at Uncle Hugo's house. Rolph was very relieved and he thanked Hans over and over.

Now it would be easier for Rolph to make future plans. He decided to stay in Helsinki and look for work as soon as possible. He had completed three out of the four years at the Institute of Technology, but since the school had been bombed it would be impossible to finish his studies here. Perhaps later he could find a school to complete his work. Until that time, he would work here. He was needed.

Rolph continued to volunteer his services to the Anti-aircraft Service, hoping that sooner or later he could find other work as well. The building where he had been living, with his college friend Ray, was bombed, so he set out to find a new place. They were fortunate enough to find something only a few doors down from the apartment where I lived. I felt more comfortable knowing that Rolph was so close. Now we could wait for the developments together.

CHAPTER 13
A Mockery of Christmas

There was so much snow that winter. Due to the lack of workers the streets were almost always snowbound. We often found ourselves wading and floundering through deep drifts, and at night it was particularly hazardous since the only light we had was from the moon and stars. There were traffic accidents and a frightening number of crimes. Martial law didn't seem to have any effect on the crime rate.

Christmas came. The Holy Night brought no joy to most of us, however. The newspapers were full of bad news and long casualty lists. Nearly every day one could find familiar names on the list of those killed in action. We lived from day to day, fearing the future, each day facing new sorrow and grief.

We had hoped to spend the holidays quietly but that was not to be. The enemy forced us to stay in the bomb shelter for seven hours. That night there was no chance to have anything that even resembled a Christmas celebration. Rolph was called to the Anti-aircraft Service and spent all of his time there.

In the dark of the cellar my thoughts went back to Harri and my mother. I missed them both so much. A few half-burned candles still gave a flickering light. I took out the picture of Harri I always had with me. He sat there in a navy blue sailor suit with gold anchor buttons and white collar, looking so innocent and happy. At least he wasn't starving in Lohja and didn't have to sit in bomb shelters constantly. Helsinki was taking the brunt of the Russian attacks. I thought of snowy winters past, with Harri and I making snowmen, like the one we had made with a black top hat and a carrot nose— and there were breezy sleighrides and ski runs. I could still see him with his tiny skis and poles, struggling ahead. The precious memories brought tears to my eyes.

But now a distant bomb interrupted my thoughts. "Peace on earth, good will towards men. . . . " The explosions mocked us, almost as if they were making every effort to obliterate all good thoughts from our minds. No candles were glowing, no church bells ringing. They left no room for the spirit of Christmas.

A sudden cry interrupted my daydreaming. A young, beautiful girl in her twenties had been brought to our shelter from the street. She had tried to kill herself with a knife. Apparently she had just received word that her fiance had been killed in action and her cries and screams were echoing dreadfully against the stone blocks of the cellar. She was waving her arms and tearing at her hair. Had she lost her mind? I thought of sister Lea and began to shiver. What would become of all of us?

CHAPTER 14
The Pitiful End of the War

In January I received a letter from my stepbrother Kai from the front telling me of the horrifying experiences he and his comrades had to face. With many other college students he had volunteered and now he had an order telling him to move out with a ski troop the following day to Aanislinna, where they should try to penetrate through enemy lines. I knew how small his chances were for survival and I trembled at the thought of losing him.

In the middle of February I met my young cousin Matti Linna, who had just returned from the front on a short leave. With his brother, Eric, he had tried to get through enemy lines and only he had come out of it alive. He was full of the same kinds of horror stories that so many people were reporting. I was particularly appalled at the knowledge that the enemy was not sparing anyone, not even the women volunteers of the Lotta Svard organization, who were being raped and maimed in great numbers. To think I had considered doing such volunteer work!

Refugees, carrying loads of belongings, were arriving from the East day and night. They had all been forced to leave their homes and properties behind. Many Karelian farmers had loaded their goods on horsedrawn sleighs and herded their cattle ahead of them into the bigger towns and cities. Finding shelter was nearly an impossibility for most of them, and they were found begging from door to door. Most of the cattle were slaughtered for food. There was so much bitterness.

My aunt Sylvi had lost two homes in East Finland, close to the border, and the words I remember her saying so often after the bombings I'm sure were the words of so many Finns who lost their land: "If I could only get back that piece of land, I would gladly start all over again." But much of eastern

Finland was grabbed up by the Russians and lost forever.

Viipuri, the capital of Karelia (eastern Finland) was a romantic old city, where I often visited while living nearby. Now it was in ruins and in Russian hands. There had been idyllic parks and beautiful, old Romanesque architecture. I remember the park of Monrepos with its Japanese arched bridges and the elegant Temple of Neptune. It reminded me of a fairyland, that vernal park looked so enchanting to me. The weeping birch tree drooped over an idyllic little pond covered with red and white water lilies. One could sink in the rhythm of that place and listen to the eternal music of Nature.

The city had many cobblestone streets and old, old structures that dated earlier than those of Helsinki. Viipuri had been the site of some of the earliest operas in Europe and its theaters were very popular while I was growing up. But after the fall of 1939, that was to be no more.

For the first time in modern warfare the Finnish Army used special ski-troops (dressed in white on skis) which gave them an advantage in mobility and unseen maneuverability. Throughout the extreme winter cold our boys fought courageously. Supplies of winter clothing and food were not sufficient, yet the men didn't question why or how. The older men were being called to take up arms and, where the son had fought before, now the father followed in his footsteps. There was no giving up long as ammunition lasted.

My brave little fatherland fought Russia to a standstill in the spring of 1940. When the Red soldiers were sent to battle in long columns, my countrymen allowed them to move in and then ambushed them by the tens of thousands on narrow forest roads where they were unable to fight back.

Thus went January and February.

After losing over one million men our enemy made a peace offer. Our delegates went to Moscow to negotiate a peace settlement. All of us shook in apprehension. What would be the terms of the peace?

On March 12, 1940, the agreement was signed. Oh, what a day of sorrow. The radio told us the harsh terms and the whole city grieved. Nowhere could you see a happy face. Our beloved blue and white flag hung at half-mast. Not only in Helsinki but all over the country there was grieving, and still it had been our only possibility, for our little country had already suffered many major defeats in spite of the fact that our soldiers had fought so valiantly. The number of dead and wounded was seemingly endless.

The soldiers began to return from the front. People waited for their own sons and fathers. In the very last hours of the fighting many more soldiers had died, and it had gone unreported. We all waited in fear, knowing that the inaccurate reports meant nothing.

I was one of those who received a black-edged telegram during those last hours. My dear half-brother Kai had been killed. He was one of those wounded soldiers that had to be left behind in the retreat. There just wasn't enough help to give them immediate aid and he was found later, his body badly battered. The Russians had spared no one.

I was grief-stricken and found it hard to believe and was becoming more and more bitter. When would it all stop? But one human life in the carnage of war is but a drop in the ocean that the waves toss on the rocky shore.

All over my country, at thousands of cemeteries, stood sorrowing people. They had struggled and died in unity. Sleep, my dear brother, sleep well!

CHAPTER 15
Farewell to Finland

The war was seemingly at an end, and the bombings had ceased. Oh, blessed relief, no screaming of the sirens. The munitions factory where Rolph and I had worked was moved back to the city and we volunteers were laid off. We were now forced to face the question of our future.

It was Rolph's feeling that the only logical place for him to finish his studies was Germany. So many technical schools were open there and invitations to come to Germany to study were still heard on the radio. After much deliberation it was decided. He would say goodbye to Finland and join his parents.

My decision was not that easy. What about my son? My little darling, Harri? How could I leave, and still hope to get him back? Without the war I would have been already teaching and earning my own salary which would help justify my rights to Harri. As it was, now I was penniless and jobless. Perhaps Germany could offer me a better future as well. Perhaps I could continue my voice training, which had been started at the Sibelius Academy. And maybe some day I could sing in the opera there, and give concerts. And Rolph was promising he would help me as best he could. My stepfather's words could still be heard, "You cannot, must not fight for the ownership of your son. You have nothing to offer him . . . " I knew I'd have to go to Germany, where there was a chance to offer Harri something for the future.

It would be several months before all necessary papers could be collected. Rolph, being a citizen of Estonia, was able to make his arrangements more easily than I. It seems there was a restriction on Finnish citizens leaving the country and I didn't qualify for an exit visa. People suggested that we get married, and although we had originally planned to get married in Germany, we felt compelled to do so now, before leaving Finland.

Our civil marriage was performed at the Helsinki Town Hall on May 30, in the presence of my Aunt Moster-Sylvi and Uncle Hannes. This was more or less a formality to help us get our visas and we still planned to have a real wedding when we joined Rolph's parents.

Finally we were informed of a boat leaving for Germany the following day and we found ourselves packing furiously. The furniture and personal belongings which I couldn't take with me I gave away to friends. Much of it I would be needing later, but there was no choice.

That night I couldn't sleep. Lying awake I was filled with so many thoughts. How would the trip be across the mined Baltic Sea? What would our final destination be? Would we ever reach it? The next morning, a beautiful autumn day, we drank a last farewell cup of ersatz coffee at my Aunt Sylvi's home with friends and then we all drove to the dock.

The bell sounded for boarding all too soon, and with one last embrace, we hurried up the narrow plank. We then waved farewell to our friends and Finland for the last time. I stood beside Rolph waving my handkerchief and tried to look cheerful. I was really leaving my homeland and I couldn't hold back my tears. Rolph put his arms about me reassuringly and said; "We'll be back again, Dear; we'll be back to get Harri." I broke into sobs upon hearing Harri's name and felt so desolate. I was leaving everything dear to me behind: my son, my country, and my mother's grave.

Suddenly I saw the familiar figure of my stepfather in my mind, his image. He looked so strong and determined and reminded me of a tyrant from years past. When I thought of the many years with him, I felt divided. There had been many happy times in my childhood, that was true, but I could still vividly hear his words to me when I reached out to him for help: "You have nothing and you are nothing!" Those words were indelibly printed in my mind and had left a permanent scar in me. But who was he to lead my life so sternly, and who was I not to rebel against it? Never did I dare to speak a word or take a step against his will. I was always too frightened. More than ever before I felt that his image would always remain with me—following, haunting—as long as I would live. I was still weak and scared and had nothing to offer my child; but now that I was leaving, I felt free to grow on my own and prove to him and to myself that I could be something, be a strong and independent person. And I will return to get my son!

Slowly the familiar shores faded from view, those beloved, now battered buildings and rows of blackened houses. Far away in the distance a familiar fountain kept splashing its way. I saw the indistinct shape of the majestic arched roof of the Great-church, fading into the distance. . . .

The freighter glided forward, gradually gathering speed. The wind felt cold on my tear-dampened face as I waved farewell to my childhood cradle. I would miss the rush of its rapids and the whisper of its pines.

CHAPTER 16
Immigrants

It was a dismal, cold, and stormy five-day trip. There was a great deal of seasickness due to the stormy weather, and people looked weak and pale at journey's end. While en route we came across what appeared to be a customs inspection boat, and everyone felt anxious, wondering if something had gone wrong with his or her papers. We saw a huge pillar of smoke over the horizon on the third day and learned that a ship had hit a mine and sunk. The passengers, who were refugees from the Baltic countries, were lost in the explosion. This news only served to heighten the anxiety everyone already felt about being on that boat.

When we reached Stettin we were greeted with the news that Rolph's parents had moved on to Poznan City, Poland, where Rolph's father had found a good job, and we were expected to follow them. Not knowing what else we could do, we continued our travels by train, feeling weary and depressed about the unknown future.

At the outset of our last leg of the journey the train was full of passengers, but later, on reaching the border of Poland and Germany, we found that very few remained. There were so many inspections I lost track of the number, and I cringed at the thought that this might be what we would have to live with in our new found home. I hoped that I could become accustomed to it.

On crossing the Polish border it was startling to see how much the scenery had changed. Whereas the countryside had been lush and varied in Germany, the Polish countryside seemed monotonous. On each side of us we saw only low, almost treeless plains with only a few sandy hills and small bushes. I missed the lakes and forests so abundant in Finland. Poland looked so poor to us. Where there once had been grain fields, we saw only dried brush and sand, and instead of thriving farms with sturdy buildings and well-fed cattle, we saw only ramshackle and neglected structures and a few skinny cows. Only the goats, geese, and ducks wandering on the roadsides seemed in abundance. But then I remembered that Poland had lost its independence and been kicked around by other countries several times before. No wonder they had lost their interest in taking care of their land.

At last we arrived in Posen (Poznan).

We craned our necks from afar looking for a familiar face in the crowd and there they were! Joy was unbounded as we embraced and exchanged greetings. Numerous questions flew back and forth so fast we hardly had time to answer them. We were conversing in German, which I had studied in college, but I wasn't adept at it yet. It is a language that I considered a bit stiff, or formal, if you will. But it wasn't long before I was fairly fluent in it, and soon thereafter it became the mandatory language in Poland because of the German occupation there.

My hopes for a better life in Poland were soon dampened by the sights that greeted us in Poznan City. As we rode down the street we saw that house after house stood empty and neglected. When the Germans had begun the occupation of the city, I was told, the SS troops had routed family after family out of their homes and shipped many off to parts unknown. The Polish people's faces reflected pain and suffering as well, and what else could one expect when they were deprived of the freedom we took for granted in our everyday lives.

On both sides of the streets I saw large warehouses, and upon inquiring as to their use, I was told they were filled with the household goods of those Poles who had been driven by the SS troops from their homes to unknown destinations. They were now available at bargain prices to anyone other than a Pole.

We passed through a park which had been demolished. It had been a Jewish cemetery and the occupation troops had torn open grave after grave, exposing skeletons and coffins, and had savagely thrown bones in all directions. On the barred fence that enclosed the area human skulls were sitting, grinning gruesomely at passersby. It made me shiver. But when spring came the colorful wild flowers spread all over the area and made it look like a mockery.

Our home, which we shared jointly with Rolph's parents, was near the old cemetery. A Polish family had lived there before us but they had been thrown out. It was a tall, gloomy, gray stone structure with a labyrinthine interior and my spirits weren't helped by its appearance. It would be our home for two years. The only thing I found enjoyable about the home were the grand piano and the Stradivarius violin left there by its previous owners.

It wasn't easy to settle into a routine in Poznan. All foreigners had to report their every move. We had to secure passes, residence permits, and ration cards—and with great difficulty. Those of us with foreign cards could not receive the same portions of food as those who held German cards, and in all stores the German card holder received preferred service over us. We felt exceptionally lucky at having acquainted ourselves with a restauranteur who, for a good price, assisted us in securing certain foods without a ration card.

It seemed we were constantly being questioned and our cards inspected by police. If we foreigners went out after six o'clock in the evening we had to secure a special permit. No Poles were allowed to go out in the evening. We were constantly hearing of street fights between the Germans and the Poles, so it was questionable whether the curfew was having an effect at all. It wasn't safe going anywhere after dark, and the black-out law in force didn't help matters at all. It was so dark that, when there was no moon, we had trouble finding our way anywhere. Some people even had phosphorus-covered buttons on their clothes to prevent any human collisions in the night.

Rolph's mother, Mutti, and I made a daily shopping trip into town while Rolph helped his father in the office where he had obtained a job. I first looked at the store windows with wonder and cried out, "Can we really buy all that?" But I soon learned that the items displayed were samples of what had been available in the past. I was greeted with an even greater surprise when I first saw into what state most grocery stores had fallen. Floors were filthy and so were the walls, what you could see of them, for they were covered with a number of posters reading, "Down with the Jews," "The Jews are our curse. They bring us destruction and bad luck," "Every foreigner might be a spy," and, of course, "Heil Hitler."

One day Mutti and I picked up groceries for seven days, after waiting in line for a long while. Using our ration cards we purchased four soup cubes, a half-pound of farina, a half-pound of sugar, two loaves of black bread, a bag of potatoes, a half-pound of fat, a half-pound of ersatz coffee, a small bag of salt, and ten white rolls. As the saleslady threw the latter into a paper bag it slipped from her hand and the rolls fell to the filthy, wet cement floor. The house dog sprang up from the corner to catch one of them but was kicked aside, and one by one the clerk picked up the rolls blowing the dirt off and droping them back into the bag. After that she went to get us some skim milk which was stored in large open cans and stuck her arm down into the container and came up with a dripping dipper of milk which she poured into Mutti's glass jar while excess milk ran through her dirty fingers back into the dipper. This was all I could take and I grabbed the grocery bag from the counter and hurried outside to wait for Mutti. Her only comment to me when she saw the look of disbelief on my face was, "Don't worry, Vikki, you'll get used to this. Hunger teaches you."

The large Jewish ghetto with its high barbed wire fence was also a very depressing sight. Within the enclosure, just a few blocks long, we saw black clad figures walking about, all with a large yellow star on their backs. The Jews were squeezed in a very small area, several families in the same dwelling, and they were completely isolated from the rest of the world. No wonder they glared angrily and hungrily at us passing by. A queer feeling came over me. I had seen animals in a zoo—but what were these humans doing in cages? It seemed that I could see revenge in their glowering faces. Somehow I felt that the day of vengeance would surely come. I felt pity and compassion for them.

Five years later those who had persecuted the Jews found no protection from the avengers.

I also witnessed numerous beatings of the Poles and heard of the excessive punishments they had received at the hands of the military police, the "Parrots" as the uniformed Nazi officers were called by the Poles. The Germans gave them few rights, and the penalty for any opposition was death. Long lists of names appeared daily on the large, red execution bulletin board, which was displayed prominently and served as a warning to all.

Forced labor was instituted, and every Polish man and woman between the ages of fourteen and sixty-five had to work at whatever job was assigned them, receiving menial wages in return. The Poles were also restricted to third-class rail cars and the last street car in the line. They were forced to use the German language when making any purchases and if they could not do so, they were denied their purchases. My blood boiled many a time when I saw the savage mistreatment and ridiculous restrictions, but I learned to keep my mouth shut.

One day while on the way shopping with Mutti we heard a parade approaching. A troop of black uniformed SS men were marching toward us. These SS home front troops were called by the people "Beer SS" because they spent most of their time over beer glasses and made it a show in order to keep the populace under control. There was a law that everyone whom the troops passed, had to greet them with "Heil Hitler" by raising the right hand. The Poles were ordered to take their hats off and bow low. An old Polish man leaning on a cane crossed the street at that time and he seemed oblivious to all in his weary progress. Suddenly a whip lash whistled through the air and the aged one fell on the cobblestoned street.

"Lift your hat, you pig," screamed a loud voice from the troop, as they kicked him out of their way.

"Oh, Mutti," I cried, "Come, hurry! Let's get away from this. I can't bow before those barbarians."

Bidding me to watch my tongue she turned homeward. "You must get used to it, Vikki—it happens every day."

Two weeks after we crossed the border of Poland we had a religious marriage ceremony, and we spent many days preparing for it. We were happy to know that extra rations would be allowed for weddings and such. This, plus what we had managed to hoard, promised to provide an adequate feast.

There was much gaiety and laughter those days in our household in spite of the war situation, as we made plans for creating a festive atmosphere out of almost nothing. A borrowed tablecloth, borrowed silver, donated candles, wildflowers, and many makeshift decorations transformed the little apartment in our big house. But we were grateful for even a semblance of what we would have had a few years ago and we were so happy.

Two and a half weeks after our civil ceremony in Finland we were finally truly wed. For the first time in many years I felt good, smart, and pretty, as I received compliments and reassurances from Rolph and his parents about my efforts and my skills. And Rolph was so strong, yet so tender and affectionate, that I could almost forget there was a war going on nearby and suffering and misery right outside our door. When Rolph was by me, little by little I started to lose the fear that I had experienced throughout my youth.

Now I was his and he was mine and we wanted to live happily ever after.

CHAPTER 17
Brief Honeymoon

The morning after the wedding, we left on a short honeymoon to Breslau, Germany. It was a cold and cloudy winter day and it began to snow. The train was unheated and I caught a bad cold upon our arrival in Breslau, and I ran a high fever. It was almost impossible to find a room having arrived so late at night. We wandered all over the city in a storm looking for a place. Every place was full.

We had almost given up hope when we found a small room in a back street hotel. Rolph went to get medicine for my cold and I got into bed feeling dizzy and miserable. Just when the medicine started to take effect the sirens began to scream. "Quickly, into the cellar," a voice urged from behind our door. There was nothing to do but dress quickly and hurry down.

The basement was damp and cold and became almost unbearable for me. We tried to return to our room but were ordered back into the basement. In the distance we could hear the rumble of bursting bombs and the whistling of grenades, but I couldn't bring myself to a clear enough state of mind to worry about it.

Finally there was an "all clear." The tension eased as everyone filed back to their rooms. The night was a difficult one for me, however. My fever went higher and I got little rest. The bombing attacks recurred two more times that night. I felt so sorry for poor Rolph. This was our honeymoon.

We had chosen Breslau for our honeymoon because Rolph wanted to apply at the Technical College there. He was determined to get his degree. While I lay sick in bed, he registered at the college and then rushed back with the news that he would be receiving full credit for his work in Helsinki Poli and would have only one year to go for his degree as an engineer.

After four gray, depressing days in Breslau, we returned home to Poznan. There we faced a new problem, namely, how to make a living from here on and make enough money for Rolph's college as well. Grauchen, his father, helped us out by offering Rolph some work in his office until he was to leave for college. He could help by typing correspondence and taking care of some other office matters.

Several months had gone by without a word from Finland. I worried about Harri and his whereabouts and I missed him so. But nobody wrote to me about him. The ties between my stepfather and myself were severed and I never heard from him.

Everything seemed to be working out well for us when Rolph's father received a notice that all business connections would be terminated. That meant he could no longer hope to make a living in his engineering business and would have to find new work. After much deliberation he decided to open up a business selling elevators, but because of the lack of materials he was never able to make that business as lucrative as he would have liked. Nevertheless he managed to make a living. Now Rolph had to get a loan in order to make it through school and that was not enough for the two of us to live on, so I decided to find a job to bring in the extra income. As soon as he left for school I started looking for work.

But it wasn't easy for a foreigner to find something suitable. I couldn't speak the German language well enough to get a teaching position at the time, so I had to look for something less desirable. Eventually I landed a job with two dentists and became an assistant and receptionist. It wasn't the most pleasant environment since they were rather surly with patients, and I found the work to be more than a person could do in a day.

Rolph was concerned for me when he found out how hard I worked. On Sundays, I threw myself on the bed when I came home at night and didn't get up until it was dinner time. Sometimes I dreamed of the grinning skulls which Dr. Hartman had as the decor in the waiting room. In my dreams they seemed to dance around me to the tune of the drill, grinning hideously. Would I ever get used to the place? Was this what it was like to earn a living? I had been spoiled in my youth, protected from manual labor by parents and maids. This was all new to me.

After four months with my first job I resigned. I hadn't been able to get used to the workload. After a short period of rest, however, I was back on the streets looking for another job. This time I took a position as a secretary with a large auto repair firm, which had been evacuated from the Baltic states. The pay was better and the hours shorter. I accepted the job offer with joy and began to work with new ambition. It wasn't long before my hopes for a long and satisfactory work experience were dashed, however. My supervisor, Erich Mueller, turned out to be less than desirable, big and fat, and with a dirty mouth. And with very little self-control when it came to women. He made numerous passes at me and made my days there tense and miserable. I threatened to quit unless this lewd behavior stopped. After a period the man learned to leave me alone.

Now and then I was urged by friends to continue my musical career. With the help and supervision of Mrs. Pick, an opera singer, and a refugee from Estonia, I studied every night after work. She was big and husky, but could sing as a lark, and helped me a great deal. She gave me lot of hope and encouragement, and finally there came an opportunity to audition for a part in an opera. It was the spring of 1941, and the place was the Reichsgau Theater in Poznan. I auditioned and the capella director, Mr. Schroeder, seemed interested. He gave me his own German version of an opera and asked me to learn some of the parts in German. Up to that time I had sung all my arias in Italian. I went home to practice.

After a great deal of practice and praying I tried again. I was accepted by the director into the company and was told to be available for the next engagement starting in the fall of 1941. I was ecstatic! I had made it. I had achieved a long-dreamed-of-goal, to make music my career. The footlights, the music, the life behind the scenes. I couldn't wait. A new phase of my life was about to begin, and it would be the most thrilling experience of my life.

I felt I didn't need a crutch anymore. I was beginning to stand on my own feet, having my own ideas, my own destination and my own goal in life.

CHAPTER 18
Life in the Theater

I learned quickly that life behind the scenes is work and more work. We had rehearsals again and again. Some of the dress rehearsals lasted more than eight hours. That called for energy and endurance.

Can I ever forget that first night's performance? There was a tingling feeling of anticipation and excitement in the air, and last-minute rehearsals and self-preparation kept everyone of us very agitated. In the dressing room the last touches were being put on. Here and there I could hear the sound of the curling irons clacking, and last-minute vocal rehearsals and everyone, including me, was rushing and excited. I could sense some butterflies in my stomach.

Finally the director raised his baton and the music rolled over the audience telling them much of the story via the overture. We were playing the operetta *Die Fledermaus*, which I liked so well; it was so gay and glorious. When the overture ended and the curtain rose, we were all ready and waiting for our cue. I held my breath in excitement because every gesture and word would be judged critically, but I was ready.

When the first act was over, we were presented flowers, as was customary, and then the intoxicating applause lasted and lasted. I knew then that I was going to love it more and more.

Forever in my memory will live Richard Wagner's *Lohengrin* in which I had a role as a herald. I still remember how my knees shook when I entered the stage for the first time. I performed in Wagner's *Tannhauser* and *The Flying Dutchman*, Verdi's *Macbeth*, where I was one of the three witches, Puccini's *Madama Butterfly* and *La Boheme*, to name just a few.

There was a funny incident during one of our evening performances which must have happened a thousand times before to a thousand different nervous performers. It was one of those unforgettable experiences. The ballet soloist was recruited into the army before he could perform, and as a substitute we had a very nervous dancer who had little confidence in his performance. He was to dance and jump over two kneeling girls in one scene but he was afraid he would trip and fall on the girls. Well, it happened just as he feared. As he fell, the two girls who had dreaded this moment, tried to cover up, but they rolled together on the floor, all three of them, and we behind the scenes doubled up with laughter. I'm not even sure that the audience knew what was really supposed to happen.

We were inspected and criticized both in and out of the theater. The life performers lead is not that of the ordinary citizen, and working long hours and late night hours is only part of the difference. We men and women worked intimately with each other and felt a very strong common bond which I'm sure outsiders observed with suspicion. Many performers dressed in a fashion not always in keeping with the latest fads, and observers may have seen this as a bit strange. I remember the amazed looks of pedestrians when we went out between performances to look for a quick bite to eat. There was no time to remove the make-up and we would dash down the street oblivious to the stares, but looking like a gypsy troop, as we sought out the nearest restaurant.

How wonderful it was for me to be surrounded by music, my mother's and my favorite. I look back on those years as some of the fullest and most exciting for me. I was disciplining myself with hard work and practice, and I was now earning money to support myself as well, and best of all enjoying it! I could not help but recall some of stepfather's words long ago: "If any of you intellectual girls had to work and support yourself you surely would starve to death." How I wished he could see me now. I was on my way to accomplishing something and would soon be worthy of getting my son back. Thinking of him brought tears to my eyes and a sting to my heart.

Over the weeks and months that I worked in the Opera, I continued to improve my singing, and I was encouraged to keep trying for better and better positions. There was an occasion when, with a letter of introduction from our Director, Mr. Schulte, I went to sing before two different boards in the hopes of getting an engagement in Berlin. I had great hopes of taking a big step upward in my career and even received an offer for a new position. All dreams and hopes were dashed, however, when I returned home with a contract in my hand only to find out that a strict order had been given by authorities forbidding all actors and actresses from changing theaters.

It was a cheerful occasion when Rolph came home on one of his rare vacations. I rejoiced. Spring was at its height and Nature was bursting with new life. Rolph was so wonderful and looked strong and happy. He was my brilliant companion and lover. We were going to enjoy every moment of our time together. But I had to take some time out to rehearse which he wasn't exactly pleased with, but he would be seeing me on stage soon, so I urged him to have patience.

The night Rolph came to see my performance we were presenting *Clivia* by Lehar, and I was playing the role of a film star. I was sure Rolph would enjoy it, and he did. During intermission Rolph came backstage to see me and looked somewhat smug about something.

"What are you grinning about?" I finally demanded. He chuckled and told me that two Nazi soldiers had been sitting in front of him in the audience and were discussing aloud the possibilities of getting an introduction to the singer playing the film star. That was me! He listened to them for awhile and then leaned over to them whispering; "Maybe I could be of help. She is my wife." I was flattered, of course, and somewhat amazed and I was particularly glad that Rolph took it in good humor. There didn't appear to be any jealousy between us and I felt comfortable about our relationship. I trusted that neither of us had anything to worry about.

After the show we went out to a restaurant to celebrate with friends. We were all enjoying ourselves as best we could, knowing, however, that caution was a necessity in a place where Nazi soldiers and officers were numerous. Someone was always saying the wrong thing and getting arrested and we didn't want to be another of their many victims.

Suddenly the radio blared out, "*Sondermeldung*," which

was a command to listen to the latest pronouncement from Hitler's headquarters. This time it was Goebbels. After much sound and fury he boasted "Don't be taken in by reports of foreign planes over Berlin. If that ever happens, I will change my name to Mueller." The officer next to me smiled ruefully and said something to the effect of: "Should we begin practicing his new name?" That did it.

Two officers sitting next to him failed to see the joke in that, and before our horror-stricken eyes he was dragged out bodily. The poor fellow was probably labeled a subversive agent and sent to a re-education camp.

Needless to say, we didn't feel like celebrating any longer and decided to go somewhere where we could talk without the fear of being overheard. For the rest of the evening we shared our anxieties and vented our frustrations about living in Poland.

Our friend Rita was troubled over a German girlfriend who had fallen in love with a Polish boy. He was an extra in the opera company and was so talented he could easily have been a star performer in any free country.

"Poor kids" commented Ruddy, our baritone soloist. "In order to see each other he has to walk a few feet behind her on the street speaking only when there is no danger of being noticed. It would mean severe punishment and maybe even death to both if they were caught fraternizing."

My best friend Ilse nodded and remarked that she saw it every day. "You know Anja, one of our Polish dancers? She is in love with Toivo, the Estonian accompanist. Poor kids, so much to live for and so little chance, if they persist in their love for each other. The gestapo could imprison both families for this."

"I know Anja," I cried. "She is such a darling. And how she can dance! I could watch her all day. I think she is one of the world's greatest."

"Not when the law says Polish performers may not solo," said Wowa sarcastically. "Lucky Gregor is a white-Russian, or we would be denied hearing his beautiful bass voice."

"What do they hope to accomplish?" asked Rita with annoyance. "What good is it to raise up people who hate you and plot to get you, if not all at once, then one by one?"

Rudy decided to put on some music since things were getting too glum. From his large collection of operatic music he chose some that would please us. Rudy had lived in America for twelve years and had a singing contract with the Metropolitan Opera. He was working in Europe for a time to develop a large repertoire, when he was caught by the war and couldn't get back to the U.S. We all felt privileged to have this fine musician in our company.

Wowa spoke up, turning to Ilse, and asked mockingly, "How does it feel to be a *Reichs Deutsche*?"

Quietly Ilse replied: "No different than I would under any other circumtances. I am *eine Reichs Deutsche* and I have nothing but scorn for those who think we are God's chosen people among the Germans. *Volks Deutsche* [German descent but living in Poland] and *Balten Deutsche* [German descent but born in the Baltic countries] are in fact much easier to get along with."

As the music filled the room and all conversation died, Rudy and Rita moved about offering us glasses of punch and some crackers. These, of course, were from the Black Market.

It was daybreak before we went home. We were tired and a little somber after our conversations of the night before. We were glad to see only a few people on the street. There was much less danger of forgetting to salute every uniform and put oneself in a dangerous position. But back home again we clung together desperately trying to enjoy every fleeting moment. Tomorrow might never come.

CHAPTER 19
News from Finland

The time flew. We had now been in Poznan for almost two years, and Rolph and I saw so little of each other during that time due to his studies in Breslau and my work. We were looking forward to the day, not so far away now, when we could be together again every day, in the same house, getting to know each other better, something we had had very little time to do since we met.

One quiet and lonely day in September I opened the mailbox and found to my surprise that I had received a letter from Finland. It was from Jorma. I still remember the tremendous fear and anxiety as I tore it open. What could be wrong? Why did Jorma write to me? Was there something wrong with Harri?

After skimming it briefly I heaved a great sigh of relief. I could hardly believe what I was reading and I had to go over it again carefully. I still couldn't believe it. But there it was right before my eyes: "I beg you to get our son. I realize now that it was wrong of me to keep him. Anitra refuses to take care of him any longer and says she will divorce me if I don't send him away."

My poor little darling. How I wished I could have gone to him and taken him back. Now was the time to act before anything could go wrong. I was enormously happy. I would finally have my son back, to hold and to love! It had happened sooner than I had expected, but the time was here. I could hardly wait to tell the good news to Rolph.

In my excitement I rushed to my girlfriend Paivi, to tell her about it and ask her to be my witness at the Polizei Presidium. We had to start the forms and papers for his entry into Poland immediately. Paivi and I rushed to the German Polizei

Presidium (the Police Headquarters) and received the information that I could receive a permit for Harri on the condition that I have an adult accompany him to Poznan.

I wrote to my Aunt Anne asking her to be Harri's escort. She agreed. I also wrote to Jorma thanking him for the good news, and explained that I had started the procedures for bringing him to Poland.

Then began the endless period of waiting. But nothing else mattered now and I planned things very carefully. I also sent money to Aunt Anne for all expenses. I was so happy and excited.

In one of her letters, Aunt Anne told me that my poor mentally ill sister Lea had died at the hospital of cancer, and that my older sister, Enni, was teaching grade school in Kuopio, (North Finland) and would not be able to escort Harri to America as I had hoped.

Approximately two weeks after sending the money to Aunt Anne, while we were waiting for the necessary passports to go through their channels, there began the rumors that all connections between Poland and Finland would be cut. I hoped and prayed it wouldn't happen. It couldn't be true. But soon thereafter I received a formal notice from the Polizei Presidium that no one was allowed to enter or leave the country and no letters or messages would be getting through.

What a blow that was for me! My world collapsed. Day and night I tried to think of a solution. I was told there was nothing I could do. I was sick with depression. In my mind I saw my little Harri in the middle of the bickering and fighting within his new family, feeling lost and confused, and I couldn't be there to help him. All I wanted was to go home, home to my own country and to my child. But there was no way. Little did I know then that it would be sixteen years before I would hold my son again.

In the summer of 1941 Germany had broken the

friendship pact with Russia and sent its troops to Finland. My little country was soon overrun by Nazi troops, who wanted all Finns to join in the fight against Russia. In spite of many promises, Finland hadn't received any help from other countries in this regard, and when Germany's offer came, Finland jumped to accept it. Unfortunately the Germans were not of much help in the long run, for as they were forced to retreat by Russian onslaughts, they destroyed the Finnish towns and villages, leaving only rubble in their wake. The Northern parts of Finland, in particular, were in total ruin. The Russians and Germans alike did not consider Finland and its people as they waged their war. What they could not conquer, they destroyed.

Rolph finished his studies successfully and was able to accomplish two semesters in one. He had only his final examinations to take when we began hearing rumors of the closing of schools and colleges in Breslau. All male students were to be drafted into the German army. It began in city after city. We were worried sick and anxiously sought out help, trying to find a way out, a way back to Finland. There wasn't a way. In my desperation my thoughts flew back to my mother and she consoled me by saying: "It will turn out right." Rolph had finished his final examinations when he received notice that he would be drafted. There was no question about nationality. Every male was called. We had two days together before he was leaving, first to Berlin, for a short training period, and from there to the front.

For those two days we wept together. Gone were our dreams of making a home and raising children. Gone was my hope of getting my Harri. Without dreams or hopes life seemed futile indeed. Those two days passed by like flying summer clouds.

After Rolph's departure I began seeking a home for myself. I hadn't lived with Rolph's family for some time, as I had begun to earn enough money to afford housing for myself. I wanted something comfortable and homelike, not just an apartment. Something that would cheer me up. While searching for a house I heard from Rolph that he was recruited as an interpreter and would go to the eastern front. He was fluent in Estonian, Finnish, German, and Russian, and would be useful to the German army. Rolph was sure this was the best thing for him, he said. Under no circumstances would he fight on the side of the Russians. Anything would be better than that.

I was able to secure a better place to live through my connections with the opera. It was a small villa in the suburbs. I began to furnish it, enjoying the planning, feverishly hunting for furniture and setting it up. I imagined Rolph's surprise and delight when he would at last see my efforts.

One of the singers in our company had gone back to Holland with his family. I was thus able to buy all his household furnishings and much of it was excellent. I finally unpacked all of my lovely crystal, china, linens and silver which I had brought from Finland. At last it would be used again. As a last touch I hung my mother's hand-painted portrait over the fireplace. Now it was home.

There was one disadvantage to this place. It was so far from town that I had to do a great deal of traveling going in to work and coming home every night after midnight. This meant that I had to find my way home in the dark, since there were no streetlights, nor flashlights.

One day I answered a knock at my door and found a one-armed man whom I recognized as our theater's ticket seller.

"Pardon this intrusion," he began politely, "but if I may have a few moments of your time. I have something which may interest you."

I was puzzled but interested so I invited him out into the garden.

"It's this way," he began. "I know you are not a willing

guest in this land, and I thought you might find it to your advantage to help the fight against the enemy here, meanwhile earning some extra cash and some additional benefits to make life more comfortable."

I was suspicious but I wanted to hear more. "Yes, go on."

"Well, it would involve your being a member of our espionage group. "But the rewards are worth the effort," he hastily added as he saw the incredulous look on my face. "Extra rations, good pay, an expense account. There are many things that will help to improve your day-to-day life, and this lovely fur coat will be your gift."

Although desiring this luxurious mink coat and truly needing it, I shook my head. "I'm not the one you want. It takes a special kind of person for that work, and I'm not skillful at it. Above all, my face would betray me. It shows every thought I have. No you'll have to look elsewhere."

He continued to urge me, describing in further detail the goals and, of course, the benefits. He even showed me a small revolver, which he described as being one of the benefits. I urged him to put it away but he insisted it wasn't loaded. As he stood up preparatory to leaving he said: "See," and aimed it in a careless way at me and pulled the trigger. A sudden blast shook the house, the bullet shot past me, tore a piece of my dress and then lodged in the wall of the house. I stood there in shock while the intruder, white-faced and stammering an apology hurried away, much to my relief.

I missed our Finnish sauna with its clean, invigorating glow and looked around for a substitute. With only one pipe for cold water it was a long slow task to get hot bath water. The water had to be boiled on the stove in a big tub. Most of the houses I saw in Poland had no baths at all, so one could understand why the people smelled a bit ripe. Furthermore they had not acquired the surface appearance common to some European countries of touching perfume to the face to kill odor and covering their seldom-washed underwear with a pretty and stylish dress.

I also missed seeing the automobiles so common in Finland. The overloaded trams were undependable and unwieldy at best. People like Grauchen, unused to shoving and rudeness, suffered terribly. I saw him many times start for town and return after hours of standing at the tram stop, or a long walk to town and back.

"Couldn't you get on the tram?" we would ask.

"No," was his weary answer, "There just was no room for me and I refuse to push and shove like a wild beast." What a gentleman!

In my mind I could see his aristocratic figure in neat attire standing, politely waiting for some person to notice him and invite him to come in and have a seat on the tram.

"Grauchen," I said to him, "you must learn to fight for your rights. There is no culture, no decency or human dignity left in this land. If you have to run for your life, are you going to say to all others 'After you?'"

There was no answer.

A lovely little orchard with its fruit trees and grapevines surrounded the house. It was a delightful place to sit and rest during leisure moments. All summer I puttered in the garden and really got a lot of good things to eat.

It reminded me of mother in her garden, how she had enjoyed it and tried to teach me the beauty of it. But those days I was too young to understand it. Now it was different, now my garden was like a little paradise for me, like a sanctuary, where I could be alone with my thoughts, away from the war and the depressing sights of all that misery of people in an occupied land.

How I wished I could have my little boy romping around in my sacred park. I would have a swing made for him in one corner, just like the one that mother and I had in Finland.

In that swing I learned to hear the birds sing, to feel the smell of the cut grass and flowers and I learned to just sit there for a long, long time and get into the rhythm of the world around me.

Yes, I was sure Harri would enjoy my orchard. I could see his eyes sparkle and hear his laughter like the time at the beach in Helsinki, just a day before they came and took him from me.

I was too deeply involved in my memories and they put me in a very depressing mood, so I thought of my bright and cheerful mother and heard her comforting me: "It will turn out right . . . "

CHAPTER 20
Rolph's First Leave

I didn't get Rolph's wire when he came home on leave for the first time. His train arrived in Poznan at midnight, and there was no one to meet him at the station. The only thing he could do was to go to the police station to find my address. They had all information on every household. How strange to have to go and ask for your wife's address.

And then there he stood before me, handsome and erect in his proper military uniform. My beloved husband. Could this be true? I was startled and speechless for a moment but soon lost in his embrace. He was mine. All mine!

Those were the first three weeks solid that we were able to spend together since our marriage. Those were three weeks full of light and sunshine. Every moment was precious and we tried to forget there was war. We were in our home at last and we lived like two enchanted people in a fairyland and gave ourselves up to the charm of the moment with the fear of the hours of parting. But, how the time flies when one tries to hang onto every moment. Goodbyes and parting were soon upon us. I was trying not to think about the future, but on the last evening before we parted, Rolph showed me a small leather case that hung from his belt and contained two small cartridges. "Vikki, darling," he said calmly, taking the cartridges in his hand. "I am in a very dangerous mission and am not sure if I will return. These are for me. I will never surrender to the Russians. If you hear that Russia has won the war, you know I will never return." He took me in his arms and I sobbed and shed bitter tears. The mere thought of losing him seemed unbearable.

Throughout that night we held each other, wrapped ourselves in each other. With a very heavy heart I accompanied him to the railroad station the following morning. I wanted to be brave and trust the future but my eyes filled with tears and I couldn't control them. Long after the train was gone, I stood waving on the platform and through my tears I could dimly see the shadow of the train winding its way out of sight. I was feeling more alone than ever before.

Oh, mother, how can I stand this burden?

How could anyone justify this separating of foreign families and forcing them to bear arms? Why, oh why? But we dared not ask *why* out loud for that would have cost us our lives. All who were able had to fight or face imprisonment. Who was there to thank Rolph for fighting for Germany, especially as we were not citizens? It was the most bewildering, frightening situation for two ordinary little people in love just trying to keep alive and be happy.

CHAPTER 21
Poznan Is Bombed

It was Easter 1943. The sun shone warmly, the sky was a bright blue and the air so soft and gentle. How good it was to be alive.

I climbed the theater steps gaily, light-hearted and feeling well. The apple blossoms were out and the song-thrush sang incessantly, busily building its nest. It was a happy morning.

The afternoon and evening performances went well. I was satisfied and happy with my work and looked forward to every chance to sing. There was war somewhere to be sure, but—it was Easter and peaceful here.

I thought of my little Harri, and my husband at the front. Was he enjoying a peaceful Easter and was he thinking of me—or did the roar of battle fill all of his thoughts on that Holy day? As I lay down to sleep that night I prayed the Lord to bless and protect my son and Rolph, and I was filled with a hopeful calm.

About two o'clock in the morning I found myself thrown violently onto the floor. The building swayed and shook. One of the walls sagged and the doors fell off the hinges before I could move. A large china cabinet crashed to the floor and dishes flew in all directions breaking to pieces. A table rose into the air and settled with a crash. In place of windows there were black holes through which gray smoke and dust drifted, filling the room. I couldn't collect my thoughts before a terrifying screaming began from somewhere. Then more and more commotion filled the air.

I was spending the night with my in-laws to share in the Easter celebration, so my first thought was of them. Were they still alive? I picked my way through the rubble and crept and clambered on in great fear.

The house across the street was burning fiercely. In the glare of the flames I could see a man's torn shirt hanging from a tree and flapping back and forth in the wind. From the bedroom I could now hear groans. Thank God they are still alive.

The door, which was loose from its hinges, was a struggle to open. I finally opened it enough to squeeze myself through. What a sight lay before my eyes. They were alive, but in what a condition! The explosion had caused even more damage on that side of the apartment and both of the old people were covered with black soot. Their bed was full of broken glass and rocks, and a brick had flown right through the wardrobe. My mother-in-law lay in her bed bleeding from a wound in the forehead and looking as if in shock. She couldn't speak a word. My father-in-law sat on the edge of the bed, gray and drawn, sounding distraught as he cursed the "Fuehrer" Adolf Hitler. Blood was flowing from his cheek reddening his shirt, but he didn't seem to notice it.

After a brief examination I found their injuries to be minor. I was still in shock, however and needed to calm down before I could go on.

"Go quickly, Vikki," Grauchen urged, "and see if this is some sort of sabotage, a riot by Poles, or whatever. We will have to know whether to leave or stay here." He shook his head in anger and frustration. "Oh, to be out of this goddamn mess! Why couldn't we have been left in peace in our Estonia?"

I tried to ease the despair and told him to save his strength. I dressed their wounds and moved some debris to create a better resting place for them. Then I hurried out to view the situation.

Still unsteady, I waded through piles of broken glass which cut my feet in spite of the shoes. The entire street was full of it and it couldn't be avoided. I found it wasn't safe anywhere, for stones and lumber were still falling from buildings. It appeared that most of the structures on our street had been destroyed and there was little hope of salvaging anything. I could hear people crying out in pain and in bitterness at the loss of their possessions. Ambulances were already carrying away the wounded and dead.

On my way down the street I met a man who screamed hysterically: "*Hilfe, hilfe, ich bin verwundet!* [Help, help, I am wounded!]" I scrambled in the dark over debris to him and dragged him toward a doctor's office nearby. I couldn't see his injuries but felt warm blood running on my hands. The doctor was working feverishly with other wounded and had time for only a cursory examination which showed the man was only superficially wounded and would soon be well. On the operating table was a man bleeding from many wounds in his head which were full of glass. I guessed he probably flew through a glass window. He was already near death. I stayed to help the doctor as much as I could. Casualties came in in an endless stream. It was daybreak before I went home.

On the following day our street was closed off. The dead were being dug out of the ruins, and the streets needed clearing. Many buildings were completely demolished with only blackened chimneys to show where they had stood. One of my friends, who lived in one of the most badly damaged buildings had been thrown from the third story to the street below when the house collapsed. Amazingly she received only minor injuries, but her mother was taken to the hospital with serious wounds and her brother was killed instantly.

One single block-buster had caused all the damage. Most rooftops had caved in, and where the bomb struck, there was a great, gaping hole in the ground. For several weeks one could hear pleas and inquiries on the radio regarding missing persons, many of whom, I'm sure, were never found.

Word had it that the bomb had been dropped from a

Polish airplane, seemingly a sabotage, but no one knew for sure. We were temporarily relieved when things seemed to settle down again and we were able to do at least minimal repairs to our homes to make them somewhat livable. How long would the calm last? We didn't know. I was learning to live from day to day, and to make the best of the difficult situations I found myself facing.

It was Whitsuntide, and I expected Rolph home on leave. He wrote that he was to be transferred to another war front, this time near Warsaw and would have a chance to visit me. He arrived the day before Whitsunday.

What a glorious day it was, to be in his arms again. I clung to him like it would be my last chance. Spring was at its height and we were enjoying the outdoors, walking and talking, kissing and hugging. Here and there we could see fishermen standing, hopefully, with their rods suspended over the Warte River. Lilac bushes were magnificent with their freshly opened flower clusters and soft, pink cherry blossoms were in full bloom. We had a wonderful outing. We took a streetcar to Gruenewald and enjoyed an afternoon of swimming and canoeing. We paddled up a tributary stream that flowed between mossy banks and under old arched stone bridges, while beavers slipped quickly into the water, making one noisy splash with their flat tails as they heard our approach.

That evening we went to the waterside dining room, chose a table under the stars, and danced to the music of an excellent orchestra. Who would have thought there was strife in the world! We danced and dined, and enjoyed every happy, peaceful moment, and only when the last streetcar clanged did we decide it was time to head for home.

Back in the city, as if the sky would have split in half, the air raid siren began to wail its rising scream. "The planes are overhead," cried someone nearby. But those words had been heard so many times before that few passersby paid attention to it. The streets were full of people.

Rolph began to hurry me toward his parents' home. We were too near the railroad station, which was always a dangerous, vulnerable spot. We had not reached the bomb shelter at my in-laws' house when a big bomb landed nearby. It tore down one side wall and the roof of a building. When it was safe to proceed, Rolph pulled me down into the cellar, and we had to crawl in on our hands and knees.

We didn't get there a second too soon. Incendiary bombs were raining all around. Inside, it was pitch dark. I couldn't see Rolph but could feel his protective arm around me. Some people around us were sobbing out loud, some were on their knees praying. From somewhere I heard dogs howling pitifully.

Great chunks of masonry were thrown into the cellar only a few yards from us. This closed the entrance to the cellar. Then smoke began to rise and fire crackled. Through flames we could see the staggering figure of a man groping his way toward us. He was badly burned and groaned continually, as much with fear as with pain.

Rolph had pushed me behind a huge box, but it suddenly rose into the air and me with it. I gasped, my eyes stung, and my whole body felt battered. My clothes were suddenly in rags. All around was noise and confusion. I couldn't move. Then I lost consciousness.

"Mild gas poisoning," the doctor was saying, "and some cuts and bruises. You'll be alright." Rolph had received a cut on his head while helping me out of the burning building. His head looked strange with a big bandage around it, but he was able to get around. When we got home, I found that my mother-in-law had a broken arm and had received a mild gas poisoning as well. Grauchen, Rolph's father, was the only one who had escaped without injury this time.

During those minutes when we had been surrounded by

pillars of fire, several buildings had been demolished entirely. There were horribly flattened bodies under the ruins. Limbs were strewn among the rubble, and pieces of ragged clothing on trees and boards. Here and there among the ruins human shapes moved about, dazed, barely alive, looking like ghosts risen from the dead. Oh God, take pity upon them.

CHAPTER 22
The Show Must Go On

Rolph received orders to return to Berlin from the front for further training. That pleased us, because from there he could come to see me more often. Every moment together was appreciated in those days of strife. We never stopped looking for ways to get back to Finland. We made inquiries wherever possible and felt that we had exhausted all possibilities. There just wasn't a way to escape. We found ourselves longing for my native land more and more, but now all correspondence to foreign countries was forbidden. We had no information about the war situation in Finland, nor about my Harri.

How I hated the Nazis! They wanted to rule the world. I had hoped that I could hide under the Nazi organization from the Russians, but not so. I felt I owed them no loyalty. The Russians seemed no better, and there seemed little, if any difference between their credos.

"Comrades," the radio would scream from Russia, "Put down your arms. By your resistance you are keeping this war going on. Already the Nazis who have seen the benevolent land of Russia have turned around and are fighting on our side. The sooner to bring you the benefits of Communism."

Then German propaganda would fill the room. "Heil Hitler. The great Nazi forces are cutting down the enemy and soon the war will end in victory, for God is on our side. We have many surprises yet in store for the enemy. Our new electrically controlled weapons will bring destruction to those barbarians. Stay where you are and go about your work in peace. We will take care of our people." To me they were just an arrogant bunch of unjust people who felt superior over others. Wherever they appeared they caused turmoil and fear. I hated them all. And who would survive to enjoy victory anyway?

At the theater we were playing the operetta *Clivia*. We had presented that same operetta several times before without any errors, but on the evening when I knew Rolph would be leaving on the night train, I almost bungled my part badly.

In the beginning of the play, I sat on a low stone wall at the right of the stage wearing a riding costume. The men's chorus was serenading me. When the chorus finished the song, it was my turn to speak but to my horror I realized that I could not remember the first words. I was in a cold sweat and I looked helplessly at the prompter, but he didn't realize my plight and only smiled sweetly at me. No one knew the inner shock and panic I felt as the chorus hummed the last notes. I felt a hot flush creep up my face. Dozens of times I had played this part without difficulty, and now . . . For a fraction of a second I prayed I could go through the floor. And then, I heard my cue. Oh what a relief, for the words came to me in a flash. I didn't stop shaking for the rest of that act, however.

I remember many incidents on stage which provided many laughs for us later, in retrospect. For example, on our 20th performance of Strauss' *Fledermaus* everything went fine until the third act. At the end of that act I danced onto the stage with Count Orlowsky just as the center of the movable stage was being turned and the scenes changed. In some way the shifting scenes caught one of the great glass chandeliers, and it broke loose, and dropped to the floor with a crash, breaking into thousands of pieces. There were startled cries of alarm from the audience and my partner noticed what went wrong. He disappeared like a flash, leaving me standing there amidst the destruction. I was unharmed, thank heaven, and the excitement lasted only a few minutes. The curtain soon went up and the operetta went on. Yes, the show must go on.

And there was the time that a performer, playing Senta in *The Flying Dutchman*, was required to make a dangerous jump, as if flinging herself into the sea. Usually there were four men behind the scene, holding a net into which she was to jump but this time they weren't there in time and Senta jumped down full force to the floor receiving considerable injuries.

We often had to stop a scene because of an air raid. All actors as well as the audience then had to run to the bomb shelters, where they often spent hours before the show could go on if at all. The unreal world mixed with the real in grotesque mockery.

The year 1944 began ominously. Everyday some of the theater personnel were called to the front. The opera orchestra lost so many members that women were beginning to outnumber the men in what once had been predominantly a male orchestra. This had never been tolerated before. It was a real threat to the male ego.

There were rumors that the theater would be closed and all of us would be drafted into defence work, but then came the order from the military headquarters demanding all the entertainment to continue, although there were many operas we couldn't present because of the shortage of performers. The audiences began to be comprised more and more of officers and soldiers many of whom were injured and crippled. The theater represented them with a few hours of release from pain and suffering, a chance to forget reality. They were surely the most appreciative part of our audience and it seemed their applause knew no bounds. In one of our performances we had the honor to have as our special guest the Propaganda Minister, Dr. Joseph Goebbels, who was very supportive of all arts and for that reason was very welcome to all performances around Germany.

Seeing the soldiers in the audience was to me a constant reminder of Rolph. Where was he? Would he come back? I knew he had been ordered to the war front again and the leaves were a thing of the past. Wherever the need for men was most urgent, there he was sent. But would he survive? Would he have a chance to join these soldiers in the audience, far from the theaters of war, and happy to escape into a world of make-believe?

It was late fall when I realized I was pregnant. I was going to be a mother again, for the second time in my life. Would it be a boy? Could it take the place of my son, Harri? No, never, nobody could take his place! He would always stay close to my heart as my beloved first child. But my second one, it didn't matter, boy or girl, would be born of passionate love and although in such difficult times, I was happy! I wished I could telephone or write to my stepfather, but it was now impossible. I could let him know that I now had accomplished something. I had a good position with the opera and would be able to support my children and give them a home. I had kept my promise to myself, my plan had come true and I could come and get my Harri as soon as the world stabilized.

CHAPTER 23
A Trip to Riesengebirge

In February, my girlfriend Paivi and I had planned to take off for a vacation trip to Riesengebirge, in Silesia. My throat had been bothering me a good deal, and my doctor advised a change of climate. I took a leave from my opera engagement. Paivi had heart trouble and needed rest. We wrote to a hotel high in the mountain of Riesengebirge and made arrangements for a two weeks stay.

It was a sunny winter morning when we took the train to Silesia. The sky was the brightest blue and clear. After changing trains in Breslau the flitting glimpses of scenery began to change. The train snaked into a valley on either side of which gorgeous snow-clad mountains rose toward the sky, blue-white and majestic, and the sun spilled its splendor on the hills. It was heavenly! These were the Isargebirge mountains as we found out, and they were soon followed by the yet higher peaks of the Riesengebirge, our destination.

From the tiny station of a small mountain village we climbed a gradually steepening hillside 1000 meters up, where the little Inn was situated. Our luggage followed by an ox drawn dray.

Could sleep possibly be sweeter on this earth, than in that simple bed at this sky-nest? And could the moonlit night in autumn be more fascinating anywhere in the world?

Paivi and I shared a small comfortable corner room from the window of which a breathtaking panorama of rugged scenery and equally wonderful valley stretched as far as the eye could see. The luscious green evergreen trees dotted the snowy landscape; tall pine trunks and the light shining through as if from far off and the invigorating soft, clean air seemed to lift us into another world.

The following morning, hardly had I opened my eyes, when I hurried to the window and drew aside the curtains to see the sunrise. Oh, what glorious beauty!

All was quiet and Nature was asleep. Glancing at my companion told me that she was not awake. The scene before me was enchanting. It was an absorbing experience to a novice mountain visitor such as I.

I dressed quickly putting on my ski outfit with a bright red Finnish cap. On just such a crisp, early winter morning I wished to make my acquaintance with those majestic hills, and I slipped out quietly and stood for a moment in the brightness of the early morning sun. Then I put on my skis, and with swift strokes I skied in the direction where the horizon seemed to meet the glittering snowdrift. I could not stop until I reached a point where the mountainside dropped into a gorge on one side and on the other it rose abruptly. The snow glittered in the first rosy rays of the rising sun and twinkled from one white-robed peak to another. It was heavenly! I donned my dark glasses against the blinding snow. The shadows drew deeper into the valley from where the chill of the night still arose. On the sunny side, away from the wind it was delightfully warm, while in the shady places the frosty wind nipped at my cheeks.

In the distance rose the famed "Schneekoppe" in its glory against the blue, blue sky.

We had planned to climb it if we possibly could. But now, it was time for me to return to the Inn before Paivi would miss me. It was time for breakfast.

As I drew near the Inn, the enticing aroma of fresh brewed coffee met my nostrils. Here, thank goodness, real coffee was available at a great price, as well as the "ersatz" coffee. The sounds of an awakening household could be heard, as we, ration cards in hand, went to breakfast.

Later on in the day we decided to go bob-sledding, and we coasted down the especially curvy slide at incredibly high speed. It didn't take long before we were in the valley below and in the little town. Oh, how the sled skimmed along.

Wheeeee! In the sharp curves one had to steer very carefully, as on either side were large pine trees, and hitting one of those at that speed could have meant death.

We had been questioned at the top of the hill as to whether we could steer the sled and we had laughingly answered: "Yes, of course." To us Finns it was plain as day that we could do it very well, but it wasn't quite as simple as we had thought. The slide was in poor condition from much use, icy and rough, and it required extreme skill and ability from the steersman, and no one was allowed to take to the slide without permission.

Each day we tried new attractions: ascending, skating, sledding or snow-shoeing and sunbathing. Each of them had its new thrills. The sun was so warm that it melted icicles hanging from the roof of the Inn and made holes in the snow which started small trickling brooks running slowly down the hill. The bubbling it made sounded like spring in Finland. Deep, sighing woods called us to the lap of Nature where the air was clean and fresh. No wonder it restored health to the body and soul to be up there, where life is true and joy is real. Oh, Lord, if we could all enjoy the un-taxed beauty of the earth, how wonderful it would be. Nature belongs to all of us and is free!

All too soon our unforgettable vacation came to an end and we were sitting on the train returning to our everyday routine and unknown future.

I wonder, if the warmakers would go to the mountains and meditate, maybe then there would be no war?

CHAPTER 24
A Baby Is Born

Back at home again I continued my work at the Opera until the end of my pregnancy. Of course, I couldn't play as many of the parts as I had in the past in my condition, but I did what I could until three weeks before my baby was due and then I obtained a six week leave of absence.

I spent all of my spare time at home, knitting small garments for the newcomer using cotton twine or raveled wool yarn from old garments. There was no yarn or any material for sale. Also I made all my clothes out of the salvaged scraps of worn out garments.

I longed for my strong and wonderful husband. I needed to lean on him, to feel his warmth and touch. But he was far away, near Warsaw, in the front lines, and couldn't comfort me. Leaves were a thing of the past.

As the radio on every street corner was screaming out loud the propaganda of the Germans, promising sure victory and warning people not to listen to the Russian promises I felt nauseated. But soon a new order came demanding all radios and cameras to be given to the Nazis. Listening to any radio programs was strictly forbidden and punishable. Our radio and camera had been stolen long before. This demand felt as being behind a curtain. No contact with the other side of the world.

While lonesome for my son I was glad he was not with me to share this chaos. The starvation had already begun and would get worse, and there was a complete lack of heating and warm water.

My stomach had grown larger and larger, and it made me very uncomfortable. It was hard for me to sit up straight, and the baby's little feet, were kicking my ribs and my stomach clenched like a fist at times. It was hard to understand that with such poor nourishment my baby was able to grow, but Nature does wonders.

Because of the continual bombings the only civilian hospital had been removed to the small town of Kosten about 200 miles from Poznan city. When a raid came, all patients, regardless of how ill they were, were taken to the cellars.

Many mothers gave birth to their babies in the bomb shelter in the midst of the chaos and staring strangers because they didn't want to leave their home and travel to the hospital so far away. Since I didn't want to take a chance to deliver my baby in the cellar, I registered at this hospital.

As the time for my confinement drew near, my in-laws took me to Kosten by train and then returned home that day. How unpleasant it was to be left alone in a strange town under such circumstances. I stayed in one of the two dilapidated traveler's homes available. Narrow stairs led to the third floor where I was to live. The owner, a hunchbacked old man showed me to my room. An iron bed, one hard chair, a washstand, and a small wardrobe were its only furnishings.

Oh, how lonesome I felt. Lonesome and depressed. I sat down on the only chair and shed a few tears. I was dizzy and terribly tired. Who would help me if something would go wrong. I needed my mother by my side!

From across the hall came the sound of a poorly played accordion and a strong odor of alcohol. From another room I could hear raucous laughter and obscene talk.

My thoughts went to Rolph. Where might he be? I felt if I could see him even for a minute I wouldn't be so afraid to be alone. But I knew crying wouldn't help, so I arranged the lovely flowers my friends had given me, in the only available vase, the water pitcher, and the waiting began.

The doctor, who came twice a week to this town, told me to walk as much as possible. "The more, the better," he said. I followed his advice and took long walks to the edge of the town into the woods. I strolled along little paths that led this way and that, or sat on a mossy bank watching squirrels at play. How could summer be so enchanting in such an ugly world? That little woods became my fairyland, my church, where I sought escape from the world I knew but didn't understand. Sometimes I sat in a field of wild flowers for a long time, perfectly still, until I sank into meditation.

One night I answered a knock at my door. There stood a bald-headed man with wicked eyes.

"Good evening, Fraulein," he greeted me. "If I may come in, I can show you something of great interest."

I stepped back and he walked in carrying two heavy bags, talking all the time. "You are a lady used to nice things, I can tell. Oh, yes, I can make you very happy. Lucky there are a few foreigners like you or I would have no one to buy my wares."

By this time the bags were opened and what a sight met my eyes! There were coffee, Nescafe, tea, chocolate, cocoa, saccharine, butter, canned meat, spices and other items. But the prices! One small can of Nescafe was 250 marks, about 20 dollars. My monthly salary was nothing all at once.

When the man saw my look of incredulity he said: "But these are from France, my fraulein. The best obtainable." I said nothing, so he persisted: "Have you no jewelry or furs you would like to exchange for these treasures? Come on, I know you must have something. Let me see them."

The coffee smelled so invigorating that I hesitatingly brought out a few pieces of my jewelry, which I had taken with me from Poznan, for his inspection, but I wished only to get rid of his greasy, obnoxious self.

I then asked him how he managed to get by with selling these black market goods, and he answered: "I'm too smart for them." He then pulled out two sets of credentials: "One time I am a German, if it suits my needs, and another time a Pole."

He offered me a good price for several items, but I couldn't bring myself to part with my jewelry for things I didn't really need, so I said: "You may as well go; I don't care to buy anything." I opened the door and waited.

His disappointed look changed to one of craftiness as he approached me and patted my arm, saying: "Well, if it's the price you are worried about, why, a pretty girl like you doesn't need money. There are other ways. Just be good to me and they are yours!"

That was enough for me. With a strength I didn't know I possessed, I grabbed the nearest bag and threw it out into the hall. Fearing he might be reported, he picked up the rest of his bags and hastily ran out.

The remaining days passed slowly. Finally, when the labor pains began, I was forced to walk two miles from the apartment through the woods to a midwife who then telephoned my physician. The doctor was vexed. Apparently my baby was coming at the wrong time. "Can't she wait until tomorrow, when I am in town?" he inquired. But I couldn't wait, and on July 5, my little girl was born, without the doctor, at the small temporary hospital in Kosten, Poland.

In my thoughts I carried the child to my husband so that he could share my happiness. My lovely little princess, small soul though she was, needed me, and I clung to her. I had mixed feelings of joy and grief. Oh, how I wished my mother, and, of course Rolph, my child's father, could see her. But what kind of a world was I bringing my baby into?

The following morning there came a notice from the police department including a list of names from which I had to choose a name for my baby. This was an SS order and had to be done the very same day. All the names on the list were non-Jewish. No biblical names were included. Rolph and I had made plans for a name, but it now seemed we had no choice. Somehow, however, I managed to wangle a few days before making my decision by stating I was too sick to decide.

On the fourth day, I heard a man's voice outside of my window. "I would like to see my wife and child." To my joy

I recognized the voice to be Rolph's. My child's father was here! I felt like jumping out of bed and running to him. He got down on his knees beside the bed and murmured to the little newcomer, pathetic in his joy at beholding the pretty little girl he had so often hoped for. Now there were three of us, all belonging to each other. We wished we could shut out the world around us and live forever in this enchanting moment.

Rolph was on a five-day leave. He spent it in Kosten with us. When he saw the order regarding names for newborns, he stated flatly that he didn't intend to let anyone order a name for his child. "The Nazis have done enough to me already, and my daughter will have the name I choose for her!" After much indecision he agreed to the name Regine. It was written on her birth certificate. Regine, which means queen, really ruled our hearts.

CHAPTER 25
Prophecy

The new theatrical season began August 5, 1944, and I resumed work at the opera. Anna, my Polish nursemaid, took care of my baby while I was away. We were only able to work three months, however, before the order came that all theaters were to be closed at once and all actors were to work in munition factories. I was excused from the forced labor thanks to a doctor's certificate.

Rolph was near Warsaw at the time my work came to a halt. He often made "reporting" trips to Berlin and passed through Poznan so that he could see us. Oh, how I loved to see him holding our little Regine in his arms. That tall and handsome man and the rosy darling baby were both mine.

The war situation was becoming desperate and an assault was expected from the west. The outlook was gloomy no matter how we tried to plan. There was a real fear that the war might not be stopped before we were all bombed out of existence. Many people felt it would be better to die now than wait for the world to blow up. Others thought it would be a blessing if there were a quick peace brought about by the United States even if our fate rested in their hands thereafter. Waiting and worrying was nerve-wracking.

In the munition factories my colleagues were assigned to operate machines that formerly only experienced and trained operators were permitted to touch. Each day a specified amount of work was required and no matter how long it took, they had to do it. Many people lost their fingers, as they were unaccustomed to that type of work. Eventually a new order demanded variety programs at the theater in addition to the day's work my colleagues were forced to do in munition factories. Although I wasn't performing at the time, I felt I was able to help, so I volunteered. These shows were called *Bunte Abende*, and we had them every night.

When my baby was two months old I found out I was pregnant again. "I am very sorry to tell you this," the doctor told me. "It looks like we all will be forced to leave the city soon. The evacuation could start any time." But as strange as it may sound, I wasn't sorry. This was the result of our love and Rolph and I wanted to have this baby. There was no time for fear or panic. Soon the battle fronts began to close in on all parts of Poland and all the men in the city were assigned to one of four different civilian defence divisions. They were trained every night and no man was allowed to leave the city. In addition, an order came, that all men and women over fourteen years of age, had to help dig ditches around our city. The Russians were only a few miles away. One day a week was spent digging, rain or shine, and days off were unheard of. This work decree applied to Germans as well as to all other nationalities. There seemed to be no rest now as bombings increased keeping everyone weary and on edge.

Through all of this, my little Regine grew and grew and before I knew it she was four months old with pink cheeks, blue eyes and blond, curly hair. She was a happy and healthy child, a lively, mischievous elf and seemed to know that she held me in the palm of her hand. What a pity that Rolph was not able to enjoy more of this little angel, our child, born out of love. Also our unborn fetus made her presence known by giving me morning sickness.

When Christmas came Rolph was far away at the front lines. He had been home for three days unexpectedly, on the way to Warsaw on a secret military mission. He told me that the war situation was steadily worsening. The Russians were getting closer and closer and in the west the English and Americans had landed and were advancing. A day didn't pass now without thoughts of war and horrible nightmares. Bulletins began to be posted advising people to pack their belongings and send them to "safer places." Since we had no friends or relatives outside of the war zone, there was no safe place for us.

On New Year's Eve, I took out a piece of tin, which in Finnish tradition prophesies the events of the coming year. In my fatherland we had always kept up this tradition and, even if the new year did not bring us what was prophesied, we still believed in it. I placed the tin into a heavy iron dipper, which I then carefully laid onto the gleaming red coals of my fireplace. After the tin was melted, I added a small piece of wax, which cleaned the tin shiny and bright. The reflection of it suggested the magic that it beheld within the flashing of the flames. Carefully I raised the dipper from the flames and quickly dumped the melted tin into a bucket full of ice cold water. Sizzling and sputtering it puffed up a cloud of steam as I called out loud my name. There on the bottom of a water pail lay my magic fortune figure. What kind of a fortune was it going to be? Eagerly I held the tin figure against the light and the shadow on the wall cast a figure of a wreath, which was my final fortune. An even circle of a wreath was the ever-feared symbol of death within the family.

What could this mean to me? Was it going to be my fate or the fate of us all? Oh, no! Dear Lord, let it not be true.

CHAPTER 26
Flight from Poland

It was now five years since we had crossed into Poland. Winter had come harder and colder than ever and the snowdrifts were blocking the traffic and the icy wind howled around the corners.

There were strong suggestions that Germany would lose the war. But only in whispers did anyone dare to talk of it. The spirit of the people was very low. Everyone was asking: "When will the end come?" A great many had packed their belongings and were ready to leave. I, being forever an optimist, still relied on the authorities, who were to give the mothers and children warning when danger was near.

All banks were full of people trying to get their money out before it was too late; they waited in long lines for hours, I among them, but only a small fraction of savings could be drawn.

I had put large amounts of my income into a savings account against the day when we would be free to return to Finland and build our home. I had received a good salary at the opera and had spent only a small part of it. Rolph had also deposited a great deal of his money into the account since he didn't need much while he was at the front. So it turned out, unfortunately, we had no chance to get our savings out and we lost everything. There just hadn't been enough time and enough warning.

A stream of people began to enter our city daily. They were definitely outsiders and looked queer with their great sacks from which hung articles such as cooking utensils and even children's chamber pots. These people were called refugees and with them came panic which spread like wildfire. People began to ask questions and hear descriptions of the fighting. Fear spread quickly and soon the citizens of Poznan were gathering their goods to join the streams of fleeing refugees.

I waited for some word from my husband but heard nothing. Where was he, and why didn't I hear from him? My anxiety grew every minute. Where would I go alone with my child and in my new pregnancy if ordered to evacuate? And how would Rolph find us?

I tried to banish these thoughts from my mind. Things couldn't be that bad, I kept telling myself. I often went to a neighbor to listen to news on the radio although this was strictly forbidden. That is, if one were caught listening to foreign broadcasts, or even having a radio, they would be punished. I suppose there was so much conflicting news on foreign stations that contradicted everything the Germans were telling us that it could easily have brought about panic and perhaps even worse for the Germans, dissension. So we listened in secret in the dark cellar. On the German radio we heard boasts of strong fortifications that would soon be stopping the Russians. Communist propaganda was just the opposite.

"The Jews must be exterminated," whined the Nazis.

"Tovarich," cooed the Russians. "Come to a land where there is work for everyone and all are treated alike." I grew disgusted with the conflicting news.

On Tuesday, January 20, 1945, Rolph returned.

"I came to help you get out of this trap and thought you might already be gone," he said. "Can't you see how the station is full of refugees? The war is lost. The Russians have smashed the German line and are only about a hundred miles from Poznan City!"

A decision had to be made now. We rushed to the "Mutter und Kind" (mother and child) organization to find out about possible evacuation. A great many other mothers were already there ahead of us. We were told that no evacuation orders had been given yet and that if we wished to leave the city we could do so on our own. We would be informed, they told us, if the situation deteriorated. Everything would be organized in due time.

We were temporarily calmed by this news. But only temporarily, for when we arrived at my friend Paivi's house the sight that greeted us there brought us back to reality. There was Paivi, with her five children, packing frantically and everyone seemed in great confusion.

"Isn't this awful, Vikki? We are leaving the city as soon as we can. The trains are packed, and they only run now and then, and God only knows where," Paivi stammered and the fear showed in her face.

From the adjoining room her husband, a tall and handsome man, an SS officer, entered in full uniform and looked equally scared.

"The latest news is that the Russians are in the city of Litzmannstadt (a neighboring city) and could be attacking us any time. The town is on fire, with many people still in it. Where are you planning to go, Vikki?"

So there we were! Where would I go? I wanted to go home to Finland, things should be normal at home, I thought. A sudden feeling of helplessness came over me. What should we do? I was tired and nauseated and the unborn baby inside of me was restless, making me uncomfortable. What a horrible situation to be in! I wasn't at all sure that we were going to get out of this one, but one thing was sure, I had to get out of the city for the children's sake and Rolph could not leave with us as long as he had his military orders.

We knew now that the chances of getting a train out were small at best. There were no scheduled train departures and the mobs waiting were unncontrollable, pushing and shoving, and literally walking over those who couldn't hold their own.

"Try to get on a truck," someone suggested.

Forgetting about food, we mechanically began to stuff some clothes into an empty flour sack and into travel bags. I opened my hope chest where I had kept all of my wedding presents and looked down on all of those lovely treasures: the gorgeous sterling silver, some of it antique, that mother had given me, the lovely jewelry and pure crystal. I could hardly bear the thought that these would be left behind. It was all that was left of my life in Finland. They were my last link to my homeland and my loved ones. But I quickly thrust such thoughts away and took out my little box of valuable jewels and packed it with the clothes. I might need them later to buy my way out of here, I decided.

Then we filled the baby carriage. I had some large bottles of powdered milk I had been saving for several weeks; they were part of the rations given to the babies and expectant mothers. I filled the bottom of the carriage with these and over them we hurriedly placed articles of clothing. On top of everything we set our little Regine, closely wrapped in a heavy blanket I had brought with me from Finland. She looked up at us with her big, blue eyes and smiled so sweetly, unaware that this was not just another outing. She was now six months old and I was four months pregnant.

I took one glance at Rolph, he looked so strong and handsome in his officer's uniform. Oh, how I loved him! He had found a small sled somewhere and now hastily loaded it with our possessions, and we were ready to go. I pushed the over-loaded baby carriage. The wheels sank into the deep snow, making it very difficult to move ahead; nevertheless, half running, we frantically struggled on. Our load was heavy and I often faltered but Rolph came to my rescue. I thought my lungs would burst from the strain, but a single question kept ringing in my head: Was it too late? Too late? It must not be, because I want to save my children.

The doors of all houses gaped open, and everything was free for anyone. People were streaming in every direction dragging their possessions, deserting their homes, cringing like beaten dogs. We didn't speak. Our hearts were too full of terror. We saw a familiar face in the now thickening crowd, a well-known doctor and his sickly wife, both on foot. We passed a sick man who groaned pitifully as others carried him along. Here was an old woman plodding along, leaning heavily on a cane. There was a mother with a baby in her arms and three children dragging at her skirts, no doubt her husband was on military duty. In everyone's eyes was suffering drowned in tears. And from behind every corner we expected to see the first Russian tanks come rushing upon us.

"Maybe we should try to get you on a train since you can't go very far in your pregnant condition, Vikki," I heard Rolph speaking to me.

I was momentarily jerked back to reality.

"What ever you think is best," I answered and my mind went back to the fear and panic I could feel around me.

There was no question of getting on the station platform since a great crowd was milling there pushing and shoving, surging forward. We stood in the background and waited, hoping to move in closer by the time a train would come.

I eyed enviously the women who stood around me in warm clothing, fur coats, slacks and ski-boots. In my hurried departure I had dressed altogether too lightly. I had on my fur coat, but it was short and getting too tight for my condition and I hadn't thought of ski-boots and slacks in the hopes that we would be back soon. Thank God I had my blue woolen hat and mittens. Oh, how much wiser I would be if I ever had to evacuate again!

Rolph decided to go to his parents' home to try to help them get out of the city. I stayed at the station. After waiting for about five hours, a train finally crawled into the station. Then the struggle began. Like a tidal wave the whole mass of people surged towards the still moving cars. They seemed deaf and blind to everything around them as they pushed forward crying out and shouting and fighting. It was every one for himself, and God help those who couldn't stay on their feet. The people pushed their way into coaches through broken windows, dragging their belongings after them. The doorways were jammed full, and some people stood on the outside steps hoping to hang on. Families became separated, and I could hear parents calling for their children and children crying for their parents.

I stood a little distance from the train, feeling the crowds pressing up behind and around me when all of a sudden a surge from the side took hold of my carriage and pushed my baby out of my grasp. My carriage moved with a tight knot of people into an open freight car and though I yelled and screamed at the top of my lungs, no one heard me in the terrible din. "Give me back my baby!" I shouted, desperately fighting to push myself forward. I was filled with unspeakable terror as I clawed my way toward the freight car.

The train began to move out and through the large open door I could see my baby carriage with Regine among the crowd in the car. I fought like a lion for her cub in order to get closer, and screamed at the top of my lungs: "Oh God, help me, help me!"

Suddenly someone on the freight car looked at the baby

in the carriage and then turned to look at me shouting and crying. She seemed to realize that something was wrong and as I waved my arms she understood what I was trying to say and with the help of others around her she picked up the carriage, Regine still bundled up tightly inside, and dropped it into the arms of the crowd on the platform. The relief I felt at seeing my carriage and baby down on the ground again was overwhelming and I couldn't express my gratitude. I raised my eyes and cried: "Oh, my God, thank you—thank you," with tears streaming down my face.

And as I clung desperately to my child, I watched the train moving on down the track. All over the tops of the cars people crowded and hung on; some fell down on the tracks and the din was ear-piercing.

After the train was gone, the crowd quieted somewhat and everyone seemed to settle down for another long wait. But nothing bothered me now that I had my child back again. I only felt an unexpressable thankfulness.

It was night when Rolph arrived with his parents. They brought a bottle of warm milk for the baby and I was able to quiet her sobbing for a while. It felt so much better now that Rolph was by my side.

But at midnight there was an air raid. On the pitch dark station platform pandemonium reigned. The bombs came whistling down and the earth shook while everyone tried to look for shelter. I couldn't believe this was happening. It seemed like hell had opened up, forcing us down into its fire. I knelt over Regine, my body trembling, and pressed the baby against my breast. We were leaning against an old stone wall, and I expected any moment that death would take us away.

But then everything quieted down. The planes disappeared. Some of the lights at the station went on, and we picked ourselves up and mechanically headed back to the platform. There were cries of suffering somewhere in the dark, and we could see abandoned luggage, crushed carriages, and other signs of chaos and destruction around us, but crowds of people in panic just stood around looking stunned and helpless.

Soon another train came in. Rolph and a couple of soldiers tried to organize the boarding process hoping to maintain order. As soon as the train came closer they jumped aboard and stood in the open door, blocking the way. Now women and children were ordered on first and although there was some semblance of order at first, bedlam eventually broke out again. I crawled aboard one of the cars of the cattle train and Rolph managed to hoist the baby in her carriage on. However, just as I crawled on a number of people fell on top of me and I felt a sharp pain shoot through my ankle. I was sure it was broken and called to Rolph to help me. The crowd, scrambling in on all fours, crawled into the train in an effort to grasp hold of something and drag their baggage with them. I had a difficult time getting back on my feet, but Rolph noticed my predicament and came to my rescue helping me up before more bodies piled in on top of me. For some unknown reason I didn't lose my unborn baby, although it felt like I might have.

When the train was full to the utmost, Rolph and I clung to each other in the last minutes before we started to move. We agreed that I would go ahead and possibly meet him in Frankfurt an der Oder in Germany. He would try to get his parents on the next train if he could. We talked quickly about plans, and he tried to reassure me that everything would turn out all right.

"If you have to leave Frankfurt an der Oder, try to get to Bayreuth (a city in central Germany). Rudy and Rita fled there and are staying with some relatives. They will help you, I am sure." Rolph stated hastily. "I'll send a message there, if I can." Our parting was so painful no words could say what either one of us felt.

Suddenly the train lurched forward. Rolph kissed me

desperately knowing that it could be the last farewell, and then jumped down from the moving train and disappeared. A cold chill ran through me to the very marrow of my bones as I wept uncontrollable tears. Please don't leave me darling, don't leave me like this! I was alone again, but now I had my little curly-head darling beside me and another one growing inside of me. Where would we go to hide from the terrible war? Where?

And thus our journey as refugees began.

CHAPTER 27
Refugees

The train stopped frequently, sometimes because of an air raid, sometimes because of damaged tracks. Sitting down was out of the question. We found ourselves standing still for long periods of time, not knowing what was going on, nor where we were headed. The night was a difficult one. The car we were crammed into smelled strongly of sweat and urine, and the damp of our clothing. The bitter cold was hard to take and I felt like I wouldn't last much longer. My injured foot ached unrelentingly and it was so badly swollen I could hardly move it, and to top it all my unborn baby was getting restless.

Little Regine tossed about in her wet diapers and there was nothing dry to put on her now. I pushed some of the wet diapers under my own clothes, next to my skin, to warm them a little. With a borrowed candle I tried to warm some of the ice cold milk for her. She cried hour after hour.

Dirty, cold water bgan to drip from the ceiling as the heat of the crowd of bodies caused ice on the roof to melt. The sick complained of the cold and their thirst. There was someone crying in a corner, and someone else could be heard singing hymns. An argument ensued when someone who had fallen asleep standing up fell upon others. We were all so miserable we couldn't even help each other. Wanting to grasp some thread of hope, I tried to think of my mother, and our song: *"Shiner sol hördes åskan gå . . . ¡All goes well, I will rejoice. All goes wrong, 'twil come right]."*

Suddenly the train stopped short. The doors slid open and someone screamed "Air raid, everyone out." The frightened people tumbled out of the cars and into snowbanks. Bodies tangled with bodies, arms and legs were flying, and everyone was running headlong towards the woods. Regine in my arms, I, too, made my way into the woods where we squatted and shivered until the planes finally were gone. Then we were struggling and shoving our way back onto the train to continue the pitiful journey.

I smelled the aroma of coffee. Some lucky person had thought to bring ersatz coffee in a thermos. Oh, how I needed some of that! I had prepared a lunch but in the turmoil it was lost. I was so hungry that I felt nauseated.

Now and then we passed long armored trains that were speeding towards the battle around Poznan. Sometimes we had to wait endless hours as the luxurious, heated special trains carried Nazi officials and families to safety.

The train stopped again and someone opened the door for some fresh air. There, lying in the snowbank a short distance from the track, I saw dead bodies scattered around. I guessed they were refugees who had stopped to rest and, exhausted from their travels, had fallen asleep only to be frozen to death by the bitter cold. There was no mercy, nor decency in war.

I looked at my baby in her carriage. I would fight like a lion protecting her cub to keep this girl alive. She was all I had now! Then a stirring in my abdomen reminded me that

130

there would soon be three of us. I was grateful that one of us was lying safely in the womb and didn't have to be carried and clothed and fed during this miserable flight.

Two whole days of mounting torture. Not enough food or drink, and no toilet except for an infant's chamber pot that some mother had thought to hang around her waist and which we passed around for everyone to use, and then emptied out through the open door of the cattle car. What a mess! Finally we arrived at a resting place: *Frankfurt an der Oder.*

The train had stopped but there was an order that no one who didn't have a residence permit for Frankfurt could get out. That was too much for my frayed nerves. I wanted to just sit and cry. No one knew where the train would stop next, so I decided to stop in Frankfurt in spite of the orders. Perhaps there would be a *Mutter und Kind* organization that might be able to give me some assistance.

I limped down onto the station platform pushing the baby carriage and dragging my bags behind me. I saw a sign indicating that a *Mutter und Kind* office was located in a distant building. With a great surge of hope and joy I pushed the carriage in that direction.

When I arrived at the office, I saw that the doors were closed and no one was there. Where were people when you needed them the most? I couldn't believe that things could turn out so badly. It was the climax of two days of nerve-wracking experiences, and life seemed so cruel. I sat down on my flour-sack and burst into uncontrollable weeping. I just couldn't move another step. My back ached and I was dizzy and weak. The baby was crying from cold and hunger, the unborn one didn't give me any rest now, and my foot burned as if on fire.

Just then someone touched my arm gently and said: "What is the matter? I was admiring your patience on the train. Why are you crying? Can I help?"

I looked up and recognized an old lady whom Rolph had assisted onto the train in Poznan. . . .

"It is my turn to help you," she was saying. "I think I can find a place for you to sleep tonight, if you like." Thankfully I nodded. It was far from the station to her home. Every step was a torture for me and I wished I could crawl on my knees to relieve my back and ankle. I pulled my remaining bags of clothes behind me and pushed the baby's carriage with my stomach. I had already lost my suitcase containing my best clothes and remaining were my sterling spoons, high-heeled slippers, a few rolled up dresses and baby diapers. And, of all things, my silver fox cape. What a waste of space!

Finally we were there. The lady, Mrs. Smith, pointed to a house and I had to crawl to it on my hands and knees. She had no room for us in her home, but was able to find a space in her neighbor's house. What a relief! Regine and I were taken care of like kings and queens. The friendly neighbor gave me some clean rags to put on Regine and let me wash her in her kitchen sink. Then she went out to get a doctor to look at my very swollen ankle. Upon examination the doctor felt I should stay in the hospital for a few days, but it was out of the question. I had to go on. How gloriously wonderful it was to be able to sit near a warm stove and drink piping hot tea from linden leaves. My teeth clattered and my foot burned like fire, but I was very thankful. Tears kept running down my cheeks as I chewed on bread which tasted better than all the delicacies I could remember.

Regine had suffered a lot from the strain of the trip. The dirty diapers had chafed her tender skin and she had diarrhea, but after a bottle of warm milk she finally fell asleep.

I shook with chills and fever all night, and the experience of the past few days kept running through my mind. I didn't get much rest, but the following morning I went out to look for my in-laws who possibly might have arrived in the city.

With one foot in an army boot and the other in a very big slipper I had borrowed, I limped through the streets going from one refugee camp to another. There was no sign of them anywhere. I decided to try again the second day.

The next day I went to eat in the courthouse cellar where I knew other refugees would gather. A meal was provided for all the homeless. When I entered, it was dark, with only one candle burning beside the entrance. Others were just being lit as I walked in to look around. A bomb had put the power lines out of commission in that part of town.

I sat down and looked around. All refugees. But did my eyes betray me? There sat the mayor of Poznan himself, with some other well-dressed men in Nazi uniforms. Were these the "heroes" who had fled in special trains with their families, servants, and valuables? Their place, it seemed to me, should have been with the sinking ship. They had been the ones to make fine speeches in honor of the Fuhrer Adolf Hitler, and now they were leaving the people leaderless, and waiting for a victory that was promised but would never come.

I turned away in scorn. I watched other families huddled together, sharing their meal. What an immeasurable difference between these and the groups of men in uniform. Where was justice and reason? It was sickening.

After a miserable meal of potato soup, I thought I'd look in a few other places. There was still a chance I would find my relatives. Among dozens of refugees in one small camp I found my in-laws. They were safe, but had left Poznan without Rolph. I ran to them crying with joy. We embraced and then after composing ourselves, talked of our past two days' experiences.

My in-laws came with me to the house where I was staying, but we couldn't stay there too long and inconvenience the kind people who put us up, so on the fourth day we succeeded in getting on a truck caravan bound for Berlin. The

Russians were moving ever closer to the heart of Germany and it was best to keep moving. Frankfurt an der Oder also prepared to evacuate.

Since there were too many refugees trying to get on caravans, a few horse-drawn drays were fitted out. We were assigned to one of these with about twenty people and our baggage. Along our route we were joined by other drays and the caravan crawled slowly down narrow, deeply rutted roads. In the bitter cold of January we traveled, passing through forests and villages, some in ruins from past bombings.

The roadsides were full of discarded travel bags and other belongings. Frozen pigs and calves lay where their owners had abandoned them. Loads must have been too heavy, horses worn out, and excess baggage had to be left beside the road.

In villages and towns we sought help for the sick and frostbitten. Often help was unavailable as doctors were nowhere to be found. Only a few would take care of those who were unable to pay.

In some places lodgings for the night had been arranged in empty and unheated school buidings. Straw had been spread on the floors and hot soup was available in small portions. We went to sleep lying close together, body to body, trying to find some warmth for our tired and half-frozen limbs.

The lack of washing facilities caused most of us to reek with odors which took getting used to. We wore the same clothing day after day, sleeping in them as well. If in some places cold water was available, we were very thankful, even if there was no soap. That was a luxury. We were all strangers on that journey, but we were bound together by the fact that we were refugees, all of us moved by the same force, the will to survive.

My in-laws were both over seventy years old and suffered a great deal from the cold and hunger, so we finally decided to stay in one of our lodgings until we could catch a train bound for Berlin. I was the only one who was able to take care of the old folks and, although the baby was suffering from hunger and my foot still bothered me, I looked after them with great concern. Mutti, my mother-in-law had frozen both of her hands and she also complained constantly about her heart. Grauchen, my father-in-law, looked tired and drawn but kept his complaints to himself. He was so good and kind and such a gentleman.

Our belongings had shrunk to very little. Only the essentials. Mutti couldn't carry anything and Grauchen struggled with his two bags. One of them, as we found out eventually, contained nothing but a bundle of paid bills. He hadn't found anything more necessary to take along and he carried them throughout the journey despite our urging that he let them go. My share was a large burlap sack on my back and the heavily loaded baby carriage.

Finally we learned of a train heading for Berlin. We were at the station early, praying there would be room for us. The conductor signaled that we could get on, but refused to allow me to take on my baby carriage. However, as he looked and saw Regine lying there, pinched, white-faced, and noticed my pregnancy, he finally relented and we got aboard. Soon we were moving again—towards what?

There was a quietness on the freight car as we moved out of the station and towards Berlin. The sun shone warmly on us and I crouched down on my bundle beside my sleeping baby and glanced around at the tired, nodding heads. Mutti and Grauchen were both snoozing, thank God. I closed my eyes and sighed deeply. For the first time in many, many days I was relaxing.

The trip by train progressed without much interruption. One air raid forced the train to stop. Planes swept close to the tree tops, machine guns rattled. Then we were on our way again.

I saw a big blotch of blood in the snow, as if to remind us of the many who had died and were still to die. When someone on the train did pass away during the trip and when chance allowed it, they were buried in the snow while refugees calmly removed their shoes and valuables. We were getting so used to death. I think we were all numb to the idea. We were numb emotionally as well as physically.

My thoughts went running back to my childhood in Finland, when mother was still alive. How much I enjoyed life then. I didn't remember the gloomy days, although there certainly were some. I thought of the days full of laughter and sunshine. I thought about how my outlook on life had changed since. Now my face showed bitterness and sadness where there used to be much laughter. Did this face really belong to me? Where was mother's happy, carefree daughter now?

Suddenly a warm feeling came over me, the spirit of my mother was with me and I sensed her presence. It seemed as if in the far, far distance her voice was saying: "It will turn out all right!"

CHAPTER 28
Baruth

In Berlin aid had been arranged for mothers and children. The station was packed with people waiting to get help. It was almost impossible to move about. People dozed on tables and under them, on chairs and benches, and on travel bags as well. Buttons that had so far stayed on our coats now flew off as we tried to push and shove our way through the crowd. Sometimes it seemed difficult to breathe, and it was especially hard for a pregnant woman to get through the resistant bodies.

Slowly but surely we pushed our way through and finally made it. Mutti and Grauchen waited outside while I took Regine in to see what was available at the *Mutter und Kind* facility.

There, in the first-aid department, I got care for Regine and myself. I was enormously thankful. I was permitted to bathe Regine in a small basin, which I then passed on to the next mother. We were given paper diapers to put on our babies. And we received a bottle of warm milk for our tired and hungry little ones. This was the first bottle of full milk for Regine since we had left Poznan. Up until then Regine had drunk only powdered milk. The nurse dressed my foot, which was badly swollen and infected and told me to prop it up on a chair while she brought me a bowl of hot soup. That soup tasted better than anything I could imagine. I felt as though I were in paradise, and I thanked God for it.

The *Mutter und Kind* facility was crowded, and therefore we couldn't stay. Many mothers were in greater need than I. Some mothers were very sick or their children were crying in misery. There were also mothers in labor. The moaning and groaning was pitiful to hear. Nurses ran around non-stop trying to help everyone as best they could.

Berlin, it soon became apparent, was the target of a great deal of bombing. In fact just before our arrival there, the station had been struck and some people had been killed. Berlin was under constant alert and people lived a sort of cave life in the underground tunnels and shelters. There was not enough food either, for such a large population, and people were literally dropping on the streets from hunger and disease. This was clearly not the place for us to stay. We knew we would have to get a train to a place where we could be safe from the bombings.

After waiting for two days we succeeded in fighting our way onto a freight train bound for a small city called Baruth, about fifty miles south of Berlin. It took us the whole day to get there. Blue with cold, we crouched together while snow drifted in through broken windows and through cracks.

Upon our arrival in Baruth, we were forced to walk two miles into the city. Our progress was very slow and painful. The snow was deep and our load heavy. People who had not fled from their homes and experienced the life of a refugee shook their heads sadly as they saw us trudging into town. They watched us from windows, pitying us, not realizing that within a few days they too would be refugees.

Arrangements had been made in Baruth for incoming refugees. We were divided into small groups and temporary quarters were found in private homes. It wasn't easy to find, however, for people were reluctant to take in strangers, foreigners.

Regine and I finally got in with a seamstress who already had one family in her house. So we were three families in an attic apartment consisting of two rooms and a kitchen. Mutti and Grauchen were sent to an old school building on the other side of town. Mutti regretted very much that we were separated. She said to me very sadly, "Goodbye, Vikki. I don't know how long I can live. Everything is taken away from me, now even the baby. Living with her was my only solace. Without my children, I am just an old, sick woman."

We clung together, trying to comfort each other and all the while trying to smother our fears of what the days ahead would bring. I needed her help and love as much as she needed to be loved and wanted. I watched her wearily plod out of sight and I asked aloud, "What has she done to deserve this? She was a young opera singer, then a happy matron in a comfortable home and now an old woman with nothing." I regret to this day that I was unable to help little Mutti or Grauchen, to make life a little easier for them in their last days.

Life was far from easy after settling in Baruth. Only one room was heated and it wasn't warm enough. Water was carried from a pump in the yard and we had very little of that. I could bathe Regine only once a week. Adults didn't bathe at all. We washed as best we could. My bed was an old sofa in the hall of the apartment. Another refugee woman and her two small children slept in the same room. Fortunately, Regine had her carriage.

We learned to do everything without lights. When the baby cried, I groped my way to her as if expecting some shadowy shape to clutch my skirts. I changed her diapers and fed her, all in the dark. We sat in darkness after nightfall and tried not to let fear grip us. All kinds of terrifying pictures came to mind. Perhaps the Russians would storm in and take us away, or rape us, as rumored. Perhaps some desperate thief would wait for me to pass by and then steal my baby. I often cringed in terror.

It was terrifying to watch from the window when Berlin was being bombed. First there appeared phosphorus balls in the sky. They looked like Christmas decorations or Christmas trees. Although we were fifty miles away from Berlin the explosions were often so violent that our windows and doors shook violently. The afterglow of such bombings left the northern horizon looking ominous. It reminded me of the northern lights (aurora borealis) in Finland.

From poor nourishment and irregular feedings Regine had developed a bad intestinal illness. She had only powdered milk and needed more protein and fruit. But vegetables and fruit couldn't be had for any price. I saw her getting thinner day by day, and there were no doctors or medicines available.

Then a neighbor, who was a nurse, advised me to give her grated apple and nothing else for a few days to stop the intestinal infection. I began going around from house to house wherever I saw fruit trees begging for apples to save my baby's life. Quite often people turned their backs on me and told me to go back where I came from. But I did find some who gave me a few apples from their scant store.

I began the apple cure immediately. Grated apple was all she ate for many days. At first she refused it, but gradually she became accustomed to it, and it proved a real cure. I was thankful that she was strong enough to pull through. And what about my pregnancy? In spite of the very poor nourishment my belly grew, although very slowly.

The Russians finally broke through the lines about one hundred miles east of us and were approaching rapidly. Everybody who could do so fled their homes, and a stream of refugees began to pass by. Refugee caravan came into town carrying terrifying news of the Russian army's cruelties.

Russians assaulted women and children indiscriminately. Women were raped regardless of age or looks. Hands tied behind their backs, the husbands often had to stand and witness the assaults. Many men were sent to Siberia to labor camps. People began hiding in the woods, not daring to return home until the hated and feared Russians had left. Many froze to death before they could return, probably preferring that kind of death to the unknown tortures of the Russians.

When refugees from the east arrived in Baruth we were ordered by the city officials to welcome them and give them aid. Straw was spread on porches, vestibules, and halls so they could spend a night and then continue on their way. The biggest problem was food. When stores of supplies were used up, and as the refugees took part of these goods, we were hated and condemned. "They should be sent back where they came from," was what we heard so often.

One day, as I returned from a visit with my in-laws, an inhuman sight met my eyes. Along the street I saw a procession approaching and I stopped to watch. First came an open wagon pulled by four ragged women and after them came scores of others. From one of the wagons protruded strange looking objects and upon closer inspection I saw they were frozen limbs of human bodies, piled up like cordwood.

The procession moved along slowly. From time to time an SS officer, who was directing it, would lash out at one of the girls with his horsewhip. "Move faster you pigs!" he was yelling. The sight was atrociously cruel. I gritted my teeth, and with tears in my eyes I stood frozen and helpless. These poor girls, apparently young Jewish women being moved from some prison camp in the east to a new one, endured more than I could ever imagine. The spectacle will remain a nightmare forever. Would those who were responsible ever receive their due?

After having stayed one week in the small town of Baruth, a new refugee arrived to live in the same house with us. She was a relative of the seamstress, and she had fled from the eastern part of Poland with her aged father. We sat spellbound as she related her agonizing experience to us. She was Maria.

As the Russians advanced to their farm, she said, she and her family loaded all personal effects onto a horse-drawn cart. Last of all they had thrown a freshly butchered sow on top of the load. The old man lay down in the back. He was eighty-eight years old and sickly. Maria took the reins.

On the way toward a safe haven in the west, she gave birth at a farmhouse to a premature baby girl. Her husband had not been seen since his arrest for anti-Nazi speeches a month before. Maria decided to go as far as Baruth to get out of the clutches of the Russians. The weather was bitterly cold and the deep snow quickly tired the horse. It was impossible for her to nurse the baby, and fearing her infant would freeze, she left her at a temporary children's home on the way planning to get the baby later, when peace had returned to their homeland.

Some Russian soldiers eventually caught up with Maria. She heard shooting and jumped down from her dray and quickly hid in the ditch. The Russians went by and continued without stopping. When Maria climbed back into her wagon she found her father dead. She was forced to bury him in the snow and continue her trip, there was no time to lose.

One day her cart was surrounded by a large group of men, who, as it turned out, were German deserters. She stopped her wagon and one man ordered her to get down and turn the horse-drawn cart over to him. He stated it was an Army order. Before Maria could protest, two men began to throw her belongings out of the cart while two men hung on to her and raped her. She didn't know what to do; if they would leave her on the street, she would be lost, so she begged them to take her along as their driver. She knew the horses and how to handle them. They finally agreed, and the journey continued, Maria driving while the men drank whiskey. She learned they had escaped from a work camp and had forced farmers to hand over food and horses. Along the way they raped, threatened with guns, and fought their own country-men. Maria was without any protection, but felt she could give no resistance if she wanted to live and keep her few remaining belongings.

When the men neared their hometowns, they left the wagon one by one and Maria was finally alone and able to continue her journey to Baruth. She arrived at long last, safe and sound. Her father was dead, her daughter had been left behind, and her husband, she learned later, had been killed in a concentration camp. What little hope she had left was soon dissipated when she learned that the daughter she had left behind at a children's home, had been sent by the Russians to a communist center for children. She would never see her child again.

Hearing this, I clung to my Regine in panic and whispered: "Dear Lord, please don't ever let it happen to me!"

Like so many times during my flight as a refugee I was glad that Harri was not with me to share this misery, and stepfather's last words to me—"You have nothing to offer your child"—still haunted me.

142

CHAPTER 29
On the Run Again

Life seemed to smile on one member of our household in Baruth. He was a Nazi officer in command of a refuge camp. The landlord who operated a store at one of the building and made his home on the ground floor, never spared insults when speaking to us but treated the officer like a prince. At night, while eating our meager meals consisting of horsemeat, brains or udders of cows, which we were glad to get, we could smell tantalizing odors from downstairs. When the delicious odors wafted up the stairway we sat in the dark and imagined ourselves at the parties the landlord had arranged for his guest, the officer. We could sometimes hear the tinkle of glasses after meals, when bottle after bottle found its ways to these parties from the wine cellar. Our mouths watered but we kept them shut. We wanted to live.

One day we saw something suspicious happening downstairs. The landlord and the officer were closing up the celler door with concrete blocks. We were told that food, drink, and quantities of valuables had been stored there. The valuables had been collected from the desperate people who gave prized possessions in exchange for food. The cellar was full, and we believed that the door was blocked so that no one breaking in would ever suspect that the treasures lay below.

After the landlord and officer fled from the encroaching Russian army one tenant vowed he would give the Russians a note with full directions as to how to get into that cellar. He knew the landlord for the insolent, avaricious man he was, and the landlord deserved to lose everything as far as he was concerned. We all couldn't have agreed more.

Now came the last moments before flight. We looked for food to carry with us. One could not buy food since supplies were so low and people were resorting to eating potato peelings and roots. Spring was here but the war was keeping the farmers from planting their crops and the outlook for food supplies was not very promising. The winter supplies were depleted and we were now eating dogs and cats, scrawny as they were, when available.

I had been waiting for my in-laws to recuperate from their set-back after our first flight. I wanted to help them along the way. But Mutti was still so weak that she couldn't bear to hear us speak of another journey. Mutti and Grauchen both urged me to hurry on my way as soon as possible in order to save the baby, and to get to a safer place for my delivery.

It was hard to think of leaving the old folks to their fate, but there was no choice left. They couldn't stand the strain of another trip. The situation was critical and I had to take action. The nights were dreadful with sirens wailing and death ever nearer. When I was offered a chance to ride in an old auto drawn by a truck, I accepted. We were on our way.

The auto could only travel as a trailer because of the lack of fuel. The car was hooked onto the truck with a rope, and as insecure as it may have seemed, I was thankful not to have to walk. The motor barked, the wheels skidded, and finally the heavy truck got started, yanking the car behind it. As we left Baruth, I prayed for the safety of my dear in-laws. Without them I was alone with my baby. What a frightening feeling, alone in a strange land. I missed Rolph. Would I ever see him again?

Auto travel by day was dangerous. Russian planes harrassed vehicles by day so we had to travel at night. The truck to which we were hooked was going to central Germany, near the city of Coburg, and it was hauling some war materials. There were five of us in the auto with our baggage and we took turns steering the car as it bounced along. We were to warn the truck driver of approaching planes by flashing our

144

lights or by blowing the horn. He could then concentrate on his driving, especially since the roads were icy. If we signaled the truck of approaching danger, he would stop at once and we would all jump into a ditch or hide in bushes.

We were passing a small, still-smoking village just hit by bombs when we heard the sound of approaching planes. The man who was steering the car at the time tried to signal to the truck driver. Desperately he tried to flash the lights on and off, but they didn't respond. Then he tried to blow the horn, but the battery was dead. We sat wringing our hands, bemoaning our certain destruction. Soon the planes were upon us and the shots rang. The truck stopped with a jerk and while machine guns rattled we dashed out into the darkness. I tried to shield Regine with my body, but I was not even sure if she was still alive. It was all so impossible to believe. Something warm and sticky was running down my arm—blood! But looking closer, I found that my arm was just slightly cut, and I soon stopped the bleeding.

The plane's engines faded away and we scrambled back to the automobile. But as we neared it we saw that its front tire had been blown to shreds. There was no hope of continuing the journey now.

A short distance from our car was a vacant building, and not knowing what else to do, we decided to seek shelter for the darkest hours of the night. At daybreak it would be easier to inspect the tire and perhaps repair the damage. We knew that the area was dangerous and that enemy patrols were always on the lookout, but we felt there was no other way.

The door creaked open as we snuck in, our hearts in our throats. The room was empty. Probably the owners had fled into the heart of the country as the battle line advanced. Glancing around we saw that their leave-taking had been a hurried one.

The moonlight shone through the window and sent a shaft

of light to the floor of the living room. The dim light revealed the sturdiness of the furniture and suggested hidden ghost-like figures in the darkness. Noiselessly we crept forward looking for suitable resting places for our tired limbs. Cold night air crept in from the door and stiffened our hands and feet. I tried warming my fingers a little by wrapping them tightly around Regine as she slept her peaceful, innocent sleep.

Around me was the deadly silence. Only the steady breathing from the corner of a sofa betrayed that someone of our group was asleep. But sleep would not come to me. A strange tension numbed me and wouldn't give me a chance to rest. Staring without moving I tried to see into all the shadows. I stiffened. Wasn't that a shadow of a human being slipping past the window? Then somewhere a branch broke. Or was it only my imagination? Then everything was quiet.

Being alone became unbearable, so I awoke my partners and told them what I had seen and heard. Then we all heard a noise like the click of a rifle. We listened again, hardly able to breathe. Then, long-legged shadows slid past the window and all of a sudden the door was thrown open and in came five armed Russian soldiers, guns at the ready! There was harsh shouting and they spoke a few words in their strange language. A powerful flashlight searched the house. Now we are lost, I thought.

With greedy eyes the soldiers made a full inspection of everyone in the room and put into their own pockets all valuables such as watches, rings and other jewelery. I thanked God that I had hidden all my costly jewels in an old shoe in the bottom of my bag.

I watched the soldiers fearfully, thinking that they might have some ugly deeds in mind for us all. I examined them as best I could, hoping to detect their motives in their faces. They had the characteristic wide cheekbones and narrower eyes of the eastern peoples, reminding me of their neighbors, the Mongols. I checked their uniforms. They were fully out-fitted. I remember hearing that many of the Russians who invaded Finland during the winter war wore rags, and had no shoes for their feet. To the victor had come the spoils, I concluded.

The searching of the occupants continued. Our driver was given a swift kick on the back when a pistol was found in his pocket. Then he was hauled out of the door and who knows where, for we didn't see him again. Three soldiers remained to look after us less dangerous persons. Presumably they knew their power over us, as they unslung their rifles and set them down within easy reach. Then they sat down on the floor around an oil lamp and pulled out a wine canister, starting a lively conversation in their native language while pointing to us. The aroma of strong alcohol came to my nostrils. It nauseated me. Loathing and fear grew every moment. My stomach contracted with fear, my forehead was wet with per-spiration. When are they going to kill us?

I had just laid little Regine down beside me to rest my tired arms when I saw a soldier rise, gulp down his remaining drink, and stagger towards me. I quickly grabbed her fearing the Russian would tear her from me. I was ready to fight for her. The child gave a loud shriek, being awakened from her sleep. The soldier was startled by her cry, and turned stagger-ing sideways to fall on a young refugee girl. Now followed a hopeless one-sided wrestle as the soldier tried to undress her, during which I began moving slowly from my place, towards the door. The other drunk soldiers were busy staring lustfully at the half-naked woman, waiting for their turns. It was a cruel and terrible sight. But stealthily I crept on. I felt a cool breeze against my back. One more step and I would be out through the door. My knees almost gave way under me, and my heart beat as if about to burst.

Now I was past the doorway and ran with Regine in my

arms towards the truck. It was starting to move away. I used my last bit of strength to catch it. Someone of our group had gotten there before me, or was it a Russian soldier? Anything seemed better than remaining there. Without a word I fell into the front seat gasping for air. I looked up, and in the dim moonlight I saw the profile of the driver. It was the older lady, one of our group. She had been sitting near the doorway and had escaped before me. After unhooking the car from the truck she managed to start the engine.

Our flight was speedy. Oblivious to everything around us we drove forward recklessly. Only after reaching a quiet, yet untouched area where civilians still remained did we dare to breathe freely. We then threw all unnecessary goods off of the truck and proceeded with our bare necessities. I was glad my stepfather didn't see me in this condition. A miserable begger, a good-for-nothing refugee as I was.

Feeding and changing Regine was very difficult. In place of cloth diapers I had to use salvaged, often used and soiled paper. For food I gave her powdered milk which I was thankful to have, with melted snow and occasionally I was still able to give her some milk from my own breast. Our flight continued until we finally reached a small town in Middle Germany. Again we suffered the degrading search for quarters. It wore out the patience of all of us refugees. I was finally able to get into an unheated attic room. Just Regine and I. I bid farewell to my driving companion and wished her the best of luck.

It was so cold and damp in our attic that the walls were mildewed and a musty smell prevailed. But there was a bed. A real bed on which I could rest my weary bones, and a blanket to warm my shivering body. I was able to give my baby a warm bath in the friendly landlady's kitchen and put her to bed in a more or less safe place. Then I threw myself down on the bed with all my clothes on and sank into a deep sleep.

The town in which we were staying temporarily was a former spa and was situated near the top of a high hill. For food I had to go down to a restaurant in the valley below. There wasn't much available, a brown gruel and a piece of black rye bread for refugees, but I was thankful for that. I fed Regine the usual powdered milk and felt we could leave this town. Going up and down that icy hill was difficult, and my pregnancy and half-starved condition made these exertions too much. The bombings continued and gave us no rest, so I began to inquire how I could continue my trip farther south.

As spring progressed the sun warmed us a little now and then. My hands had turned dark red and were full of sores from the frost bites. I had long ago lost my mittens during a raid. My foot, though somewhat better, still bothered me. A kind and considerate woman took pity on me, and offered me a pair of shoes, much too large, but sturdy and warm. My fur coat, which had once been nice enough to wear to the theater, now hung ragged over my deformed body, and its once white coat lining was yellow and grimy. I must have been an unbelievable sight and had anyone known me they might not have recognized me in that tattered state.

I was tired, hungry and miserable. I worried over the future constantly. Where could we go? What would I do alone? Where was my husband, and would I ever see him again? What would become of our babies? My money was just about gone. The three bank books I carried faithfully were nothing but paper now. Marked in those books had been all of our savings for the future. They had represented our dreams of a good life, with a home and a happy, healthy family. We had denied ourselves many things in order to save for the future. Now those dreams would remain just that—nothing but dreams—castles in the air.

But I knew I would go on and make the best of things. Mother had left me a legacy of hope and courage. I wanted

149

to at least pass that along to my children. I wouldn't give up. I had my Regine, and I would have another child soon, for whom I would work and live to make life better. I pressed little Regine to my breast. Nearly nine months old, yet she couldn't sit up alone! She had suffered, I knew that, but her blue eyes smiled at me so sweetly, and she tried hard to babble something as her golden, curly-head turned to look at me. No earthly power could separate us, never! Everything must come out all right.

It wasn't more than a few days before I heard of a truckload of refugees leaving for Bayern and points south. I wanted to join them, because it was the direction of the city of Bayreuth; Rolph had suggested to me, in the last minute of our conversation in the train leaving Poznan, to try to get there and look up our Opera friends, Rudy and Rita, who fled to some relatives in that city. Rolph was going to try to send a message to them if he could, and I had high hopes that possibly they could take care of Regine during my confinement with the new baby. I was then seven months pregnant, a haggard and thin looking woman, but full of determination.

It was in the middle of March when we traveled in an open truck towards Bayreuth. It was still cold and the roads were icy. The going was rough. The truck, which used crushed coal for fuel, kept puffing black smoke into our faces. There were about twenty of us, women and children, with our bundles of possessions, some sitting on hard wooden benches, some on the floor. Now and then the operator, who looked more like a chimney sweep than a truck driver, climbed up and stirred the coal in a round pipe. I think we turned as blackened as he.

I shall never forget the feelings that the residents of towns and villages had for us refugees. We were always cursed and reviled for something we couldn't control. We hated being refugees as much, if not more, than they hated seeing us. We represented the disturbance of peace, the depletion of supplies, the invasion of the nation by foreigners. We were without real identities then. Whether we came from riches or poverty, the country or the city, we were all one and the same—damned beggers—refugees.

When the truck finally arrived at the crossroads to Bayreuth, I left it and pushed the baby carriage the rest of the way into town, dragging my last belongings in a large sack behind me.

Spring was almost there, and the warm wind had a gentle touch on my face. Oh, God, how good it felt. It seemed like arriving at some peaceful harbor and I could almost swear that my mother was with me and led me by the hand. Could it be that I would find a haven at last?

CHAPTER 30
The City of Bayreuth

Bayreuth is an old town famous for its great Richard Wagner Opera House and is situated in a lovely wooded area in the province of Bayern in Middle Germany. The composer, in whom the town still takes great pride, lies buried in the orchard of his home. His house was struck by bombs and his tomb as well, but his memory lives on in the world of music. Also another famous composer lies buried in the cemetery of Bayreuth, Franz Liszt; his tomb was also damaged by a bomb, but people continue to come from afar to view his resting place.

In the past, big crowds had filled the Richard Wagner Opera House, many coming from overseas. The members of the opera company were chosen very carefully, and only the best appeared there. In fact, many great singers who now are reaping fame and fortune at the Metropolitan Opera, once appeared at the Wagner Opera House in Bayreuth. Of course, the war ended all forms of entertainment there.

After a long and wearisome search I finally found our friend Rudy and his family in a small refugee colony in the suburbs of Bayreuth. It was wonderful to see familiar faces again. It felt as if they were members of my own family that I was seeing after many years. Everything looked brighter again.

Bayreuth hadn't been bombed, and sitting in bomb cellars was not necessary. English and American planes were beginning to fly over the city every day, but since nothing had happened, the people of Bayreuth moved about unconcerned.

Because of this safe haven reputation, more refugees had come there than could be taken care of. All barns, railroad cars and shacks were full, and there wasn't a citizen living alone in his house or apartment. Rudy's family lived at the mercy of others, being refugees as well; they couldn't take me in to live with them, and Rudy's relatives had the house full of strangers. So after endless searching I succeeded in getting lodgings in a neighbor's attic bedroom, small and un-heated, but it was a roof over our heads.

There had been no word from Rolph. I worried about him and the delivery of my new baby, and I was getting very uncomfortable and depressed. Who would take care of Regine? Rudy and Rita had no room for her.

I wasn't permitted to cook in my room, so I was forced to go into town each day for food. With Rudy, Rita and their son Henry we often chose a restaurant called "Eule." The meals were poor, mostly "ersatz" and got worse every day. Our food cards lasted only a short while, so we had to be satisfied towards the end of the month with a watery soup that tasted like sawdust. This was especially hard on Rudy

152

because he always had an enormous appetite which he had been able to satisfy while living in America and Finland. He would sit at the table brooding aloud: "To think that I am reduced to eating this vile stuff. It isn't fit for a beast. How can you eat such dishwater?"

Regine's food was the biggest problem. I borrowed a thermos bottle and carried some cereal for her. This she had for every meal, but after standing in the thermos for hours it didn't taste good. I tried very hard to get a hot plate, but the man who owned it wanted only cash.

After returning from town I often sat with Rita and Rudy in the theater room while Regine slept, and we dreamt of days gone by.

I dreamed of my cozy warm bed in our squirrel heaven in Finland, swung from the balcony to the silver-leaf trees, rode our Maska horse to the stables and played with my puppy dog. Or I imagined eating the most fantastic Finnish foods: *Karjalan paisti, kalakukko* and *pulla*. Oh, how good they were. I could almost taste them again.

The rooms were cold, but sometimes we were able to borrow the landlady's electric curling iron with which we could heat a little water and make tea from special plants and leaves. Even though the tea had a bitter flavor we drank it with pleasure, and if we had some sour bread to chew on, it was a party.

The situation between my landlady and me was uncomfortable, and I began to realize how hard it was to live at the mercy of others. She wasn't happy to have refugees in her home. When I requested to have my friends visit me, she refused, stating that they tracked dirt in, and she also insisted that I use cold water to bathe in, warm water requiring precious fuel to heat. I tried to ignore the rejections and kept my peace feeling that we were lucky enough to have a place to stay, but when I could smell the delicious odors of food wafting up to our room during mealtimes, it was all I could do to keep from screaming. I often sat and cried with hunger.

Finally there came a day when I was summoned to the police station to be told that I could no longer stay in Bayreuth. My landlady could not keep me after my new baby would be born and there was no other room available. I walked home with a heavy heart not knowing where to go, nor what to do. I truly felt rejected at that point and didn't know if it was worth being alive. I hadn't heard anything from Rolph and now this. But one look at my baby in her carriage told me that I had a reason to live. She was my little princess, my joy and sunshine. Oh, Lord, I prayed, give me strength to go on. I must live to save my children!

Before I could prepare to leave the city, Bayreuth became a target for bombings. There had been repeated warnings from the enemy that Bayreuth would be bombed if they wouldn't surrender, and apparently our city leaders were not willing to give in.

"We will defend our city to the last man," was the Mayor's answer, but the whole town seethed with hate and fear.

Soon thereafter we were introduced to the life of cave-dwellers, as wave after wave of raids poured down on us. The situation was serious indeed but not new to me. Funny, but I didn't get excited about it anymore.

After a few days the center of the city was a great smoking ruin. There was scarcely a building left intact. People were killed by the hundreds and many injured lay buried in the ruins. Cries could be heard day after day from those left to die under the rubble.

The German army was apparently disintegrating. Soldiers had been ordered to remain in the barracks areas during the bombing raids. But after the barracks received several direct hits and hundreds of soldiers were killed, nothing could hold them. There was a steady stream of soldiers leaving the city.

154

I saw them running towards the woods as soon as the first planes approached for a raid.

Stores closed, and most restaurants as well. Food was almost impossible to find. Luckily I still had powdered milk for Regine, but I had begun to resort to chewing on potato peelings and roots of plants and washing them down with water. How I ever survived in my pregnant condition only the Lord knows.

Rudy's family and I had an agreement. They would knock on my window when passing by on the way to the shelter. Rudy sat by his radio day in and day out listening to the news of the approaching enemy, and he kept us more informed than we could have been otherwise when the news from other sources was faulty and delayed. I was glad to have my friends there to warn me of an attack.

But then came a time when I noticed them hurrying by without stopping. My landlady had fled with her children and left me to take care of her house, so I sat there without warning when a raid came. I knew something was wrong. My best friends were forsaking me. But why?

Once after a raid we met on the street and they asked me: "Where have you been? You should have come to the new shelter we go to. Our new friends' basement is really sturdy. We shall take you there sometime!"

But that sometime never came. I found myself alone more and more. Rudy and Rita had found a suitable place outside of the city and moved. They left Bayreuth to move in without an explanation.

I knew where they were so I decided to go out and see them. Perhaps we could have a talk.

I found Rudy and Rita in the company of their new friends and felt distinctly out of place and unwelcome. As they glanced at the baby, I even heard someone whisper that they'd leave if the kid stayed.

Then I heard Rita: "No, they can't stay, we are already too many here." I felt crushed. I had been rejected again.

Before I left, however, I asked permission to give Regine a warm bath, and this they allowed me to do. But when the bath was over, Rudy came over to me and said: "You know, Vikki, we all think that it would be much safer for you and the baby to stay in the city shelter, I'll take you there." The message was clear, I didn't need any prodding.

"It is kind of you to offer to take me back, but I don't intend to go back there. It is a rat hole. I'd rather go to the woods."

"Nonsense," said Rudy, "you have to go back while you can," and he took hold of my carriage and began pushing it down the road. I tried to take my carriage away from him, but he insisted and continued to walk ahead.

All the way back to the city I pleaded with him. I wanted to go somewhere else, I didn't know where, but the city frightened me. However I pleaded with him, it was no use. Rudy led the way back into the city and to the shelter and left me there, then returned. Is this friendship?

Bitter tears of loneliness streamed down my cheeks. I was grief-stricken. In my miserable confused condition I thought of the Finnish poet Koskenniemi who expressed that situation so very well: *"Yksin o'ot sina ihminen, kaiken keskellä yksin. . . ."*

> Alone though you art, midst all, alone,
> Born alone, in death will be alone,
> Alone hideth thy sins, alone will weep.
> Only thy shadow will ever faithful be.

I thought of my husband at the front lines fighting for something that wasn't his. Oh, how I missed him! And where was my son, Harri? He was behind a curtain that separated him from me, and I had no way to contact him. I could only pray for him. And what was going to happen to my sweet Regine and the child that was ready to come out to this terrible chaos? And what about me?

In order to keep my sanity, I sometimes tried to think of my mother whom I lost while yet so young. Many times in my desperate moments I thought of her so intensively that I felt her presence. This time it happened again and I heard her say: "It will turn all right."

CHAPTER 31
Traveling Nowhere

Having heard that mothers and small children were being evacuated out of Bayreuth, I decided to report for just such a migration. There was nothing to keep me in the city any longer. My stomach had grown larger and uncomfortable, and the baby was turning and pinching almost constanty. Soon it would be time for delivery, but where?

I hurried to the registration center on a borrowed bicycle and feared every moment that I wouldn't get back to my baby before the next bombing. I peddled and peddled as in panic. My knees ached and I was out of breath but arrived in one piece, procured all the necessary papers for the evacuation and hurried back.

At the registration center I was given orders to be at the station with my baby early the next morning to board the train. I arose early and had everything ready to go, but then at the last moment I changed my mind. I felt so worn out and exhausted that I feared my baby might be born on the way and I decided it would be best to stay put. I was very restless and lonesome for Rolph to comfort me. The baby was kicking very strongly, and I could feel my stomach clenching.

That night we were subjected to the heaviest bombings the city had ever had. I hardly had time to snatch up the baby and rush to the street towards the shelter when the bombs rained.

I threw myself down on the cobblestones shielding Regine with my body. The dark night was changed into day by the bright and roaring flames, and the earth shook as if it were about to swallow us all. Stones, pieces of glass and wood flew through the air around me. I could hear people screaming. A glance to my right showed pillars of fire and smoke belching out of some buildings, and on my left I saw a stream of rats finding their way to safety.

After two hours the planes disappeared and a deep silence settled in. It was a dark and joyless silence. A great deal of destruction had been wrought, and before long the cries of human suffering and sorrow rose up to fill in the momentary silence. I hurried now to the shelter, fearing the planes would be back.

I was relieved to see people in the shelter. I wanted the comfort of other people's company. Someone had brought a large thermos with hot coffee in it and was sharing it with others. I gratefully accepted some and it felt good to have something warm going into the stomach. There were also some homemade cookies. I handed one to Regine. She babbled and prattled and shoved it at everyone, smiling happily. We all laughed, and this created a relaxed, happy moment. Her lack of concern and her confidence in me affected me. I clutched her tightly, and tried to draw some of that confidence from her. I knew I would need it if we were to survive. Oh, how I loved her and needed her, especially now, because I hadn't heard a word from Rolph, and my anxiety grew day by day.

For two days and nights we stayed in the damp shelter. There wasn't a ray of light. Candles were no longer available. We stumbled over each other's feet and spattered slime on our clothing. Our feet were wet and cold day in and day out.

As the earth shook all the people crowded together trying to grab hold of something or each other. Then someone yelled "Gas!" A dreadful pandemonium let loose. Everyone frantically searched for gas masks and tried to get them on in the darkness. The children fought against putting them on, howling at the top of their voices. Distress and terror gripped everyone.

I didn't have a gas mask. I didn't think I could have put one on my Regine so I didn't want one either. I fastened a damp cloth over her face and one over mine. I was sure I could smell the gas. The minutes dragged on as we waited in suspense. Then someone said: "False alarm!" The odor we had thought to be gas had been imaginary. So great was our fear that panic had set in before we could collect our senses and think.

I had stepped out onto the lower stone steps to get some fresh air and to try to relax after the tension of the past moments. But I was greeted by a sight that caused great rage to well up inside me, making me more tense than before. I was standing by the door when a wounded soldier appeared, looking down at us from the top step. One of his legs had been amputated at the knee and now both arms were bleeding. He leaned against the wall to steady himself and appealed to a Nazi officer who appeared in the doorway to help him into the shelter. The officer shrugged and said coldly, "I'm an officer. Don't you see? It isn't my duty," and walked away.

I couldn't believe my ears. Was it possible for anyone to pass a wounded soldier of *any* country in that cndition with such cruel apathy? I wanted to lash out and hit the officer, and to shake sense into him. It was inhuman to be so cold. There has to be some human compassion among us or it would be useless to try to survive. The anguish I felt was inexpres-

159

sible. I scrambled up to help him and then sat down to brood alone. I couldn't risk my child's and my safety by confronting someone who was too inhuman to understand in the first place. I kept quiet.

After three days and nights I was so tired from loss of sleep and lack of food that I decided I couldn't take it any longer. I had to get out. The crying of children and hysterical people around me was unnerving to say the least. And the musty air made one so dizzy it was hard to think. One man had lost his mind, and continued to rave for hours, sometimes crying, sometimes laughing. I had to get away from that cellar at whatever cost.

I stumbled up the cellar stairs with Regine and headed for the house to get her carriage. Then we started down the road leading out of town, oblivious to the planes overhead.

The city around me seemed to be one big cemetery. There was so much destruction and desolation. I walked on almost aimlessly. I really didn't know where I was going. I just had to get out.

My mind cleared. I began to think again as I trudged on down the road. But I was so tired. So much had happened to me in the last few months, and even years. I felt ten years older. Where were my friends and family? Why was I going through this alone? No word from Rolph. Was he alive? Was Harri all right? Was he alive? I wanted to fall asleep and then wake up knowing that all my dreadful past was but a bad dream. I wanted to wake up and have Rolph by my side, to hold me and love me. I needed him so! Why was I crying? Why did I live and breathe? A strange question! I didn't know.

It was Sunday. The April sun shone brightly and felt so good on my back. Where had I been that I hadn't noticed it was spring? The new greening of summer was already seen in the crevices of the hillside. It was wonderful to fill one's lungs with fresh air.

I walked along the highway past a former army training ground. In the distance I could see some low-flying planes attacking a group of travelers. They were so far away, that I didn't take any precautions. There was an endless line now, of women, children and old folks moving out of the city, and the woods were full of homeless wanderers, like me, distraught and bitterly miserable.

The German army had taken a stand on the wooded side of the road. Long rows of tanks and guns were placed under cover of trees and camouflaged with branches against enemy fliers. A great many trucks filled with ammunition and food stood beside the road awaiting further orders, and the woods were full of the gray-clad soldiers in hiding. It was dangerous for civilians to stay so close to these military units, so we all hurried to pass them.

Getting closer, I noticed some of the fugitives begging for food from the men in charge of the rations. There were quantities of canned meats and piles of bread plainly visible and a soldier was distributing slices of bread among some of the children. But I didn't dare stop to beg. It was still disagreeable to me, though I had had to do it many times in order to keep alive. Without stopping I hurried on to get away from the area before nightfall.

A little further down the road I came upon a middle-aged, wounded Austrian soldier, named Paul. He looked at me with friendly eyes and asked, "Where are you going so heavily loaded?"

"I'm looking for a roof for our heads," I answered. "I don't know if I'll find one before night."

"I am in the same boat," he went on, clambering up from the ditch and hobbling along beside me. He explained that he was on his way home, and had barely escaped from a hospital before it was destroyed. He had grown tired of waiting in the hospital and had decided to get out on his own.

We kept pace with each other and exchanged stories of our experiences and walked on and on. It was somewhat easier while in the company of someone to talk to and who shared the same fate.

"Where is your husband?" he asked.

"God only knows," I replied, "I last saw him in Poznan City. My Rolph went to Breslau to study engineering and was drafted right after graduation."

"I had the same misfortune," he continued. "I was drafted, and with little choice in the matter. If I had refused, I'm afraid I wouldn't have seen my family again. As a soldier, I knew there was a tiny chance that I would survive and return home."

We talked amiably and walked on, sometimes resting awhile. Later in the day an elderly woman, called Frau Schmidt, joined us. She was from Berlin and had lost her home and husband. She too was in search of a place to spend a few nights and was reluctant to be alone.

From house to house we wandered dragging our bundles and packs, begging to be allowed to spend the night in a haybarn or loft. We were refused. There didn't seem to be room for us anywhere. It was clear that we were not welcome. One farmer even ran out with his dog to curse us as we entered his farm yard. "Get to hell out of here," he shouted. "Go back where you came from! You goddamn refugees and thieves." Still cursing to himself he turned away to enter the house and slammed the door behind him.

"Oh God, take pity upon us." I felt that the torment in hell couldn't be worse than being a refugee. And so our journey continued. The streets were filled with people with bundles.

Finally we found a reluctant farmer who allowed us to sleep in his barn but forbade us to have any kind of light, for fear of being fired on by enemy planes and fire. Thankful that we had a roof over us, we dug ourselves into the hay and dropped off into an exhausted stupor.

162

The farmhouse was a large, three winged, gloomy affair, built of rough lumber, now rotted and gray. In the middle part of the shed the farmer kept all his wagons, sled and other implements. There he also let his flock of chickens in at night and they flew up to the roosts on either side, cackling and scolding. This part of the building was only partially divided from the ends where the hay and straw was stored and where we now lived. The dividing wall was open at the top giving free access to our part of the haybarn. The chickens took advantage of it. They were our only visitors aside from some rats and field mice.

Cold air poured into the soot-blackened shack constantly through a large opening near the roof and we had to bury ourselves deep in the musty hay to keep warm. The noisy wind howled and seemed to shake our shack. I lay there awake, trembling. What was going to be our fate? The rough floor was broken in many places and there were great holes into which we stumbled in the dark, tearing our clothing and cutting our legs. What had we done to deserve this? When was our time to go? I knew I had to survive for my child and for the unborn.

My little Regine lay day and night in her hay bed. She was so good and sweet and reminded me of the Christ child in the manger. The few clothes and diapers that I had been able to beg for my darling baby I washed in the ice cold water from the well, as the people of the household refused to give us any warm water. I hung my wash out to dry on the branches of a tree in the yard but the cold damp air couldn't dry them completely, and they were always still wet and stiff when I had to use them again. In order to warm and dry the diapers a little, I pushed them under my clothes, next to my skin before I put them on Regine. A long time afterwards there were big red patches on my chest as a reminder of this dire time.

We grown-ups found it necessary to walk around outside in order to keep warm. Sometimes I crept very close to the cows in their barn and kept my frozen hands next to their skin until I felt their warmth creep into me.

Every day when we arose, we went from house to house begging for a few potatoes to eat. Frau Schmidt went to one house and I to another leaving Paul with the baby. Hunger was our constant companion.

I offered to assist the farmer in milking the cows in exchange for a little milk for Regine. He agreed and I learned quickly how difficult it was to get milk from a cow, especially for my untrained fingers! How they froze in the early morning cold! They just couldn't work fast enough.

We were disappointed, to say the least, that the farmer and his wife didn't invite us into their home. Nor did they ever share their food with us. They didn't even want to bargain. We kept our distance, therefore, and tried not to antagonize what was already a sensitive situation. But hadn't Christ said: "Ever as ye do it unto the least of these my brothers, so ye do it unto me."

I do remember, however, going into the house to get warm water for Regine's bath and smelling the foods cooking in the kitchen. I tried to ignore it as best I could, but it wasn't easy. I know I couldn't have been as selfish if I were in their position. Why didn't people want to share with those in need? I didn't understand it. Perhaps the threat of death, or better yet, the intense struggle for survival, closes people's eyes to the needs of others. I hoped I would never be so blind!

Paul went out to look for food once at an army camp not too far away. Hanging an old canteen on his belt he limped down the road and didn't return for several hours. But when he finally came back, he had with him a canteen full of delicious hot stew. We all gobbled it down hurriedly, almost as if we feared it would disappear before we had a chance to eat it. How thankful I was for that meal!

As the war moved closer, the surrounding farms became full of refugees, all camping out in barns and sheds. German soldiers were fleeing from the war front in great numbers and some knocked on our doors. They told us how close the front was, and that they didn't want to fight anymore. According to them ammunition had long since given out and most of the officers had fled. The soldiers felt the situation was hopeless. Next to us, in a shed, a minister and his family had settled in. We could hear them singing gospels and praying.

One sunny day I sat with my new found friends on a haypile chewing on some potato peelings and discussing our situation when one of them asked me what I planned to do when my labor started. What a question! Of course, I had no idea. I expressed my fears that it might even be an early delivery. Paul, always the helpful man, tried to reassure me by telling me about his experience in helping to give birth to his third child. He said, "I followed my wife's directions and they both came through fine. So, don't worry, Vikki, we can take care of you."

"Yes," Frau Schmidt chimed in, "we will try our best to help you. Don't worry."

At last a little human kindness. I was grateful to have friends in such a time of need. Although I was skeptical about the time and place, I didn't want anybody to know about my fears. I had two more months to go, so I tried to put it out of my mind until the time came, although the discomfort at times was almost unbearable.

We were now between two lines of battle, the American and the German, in the middle of the rain of terror. There was plenty of crossfire. The earth began to shake regularly with the explosion of bombs and we could hear branches cracking in the distance. Smoke hung over the whole area as towns nearby burned.

I was now the only one who stayed above ground through it all. Also Paul and Frau Schmidt finally could take no more of the turmoil and chose to sit in a root cellar nearby as did most people on the farms. I didn't fear death anymore, and trusted to fate. With Regine in my arms I laid in the hay loft listening to the roar of battle. Every so often the cannon sent a shell overhead with its dreadful whistle and whine, then a muffled boom, telling me it had hit its target. The sound of it shook my whole body and cold sweat poured down my neck and back as I tossed and turned in my miserable hay bed. The horror and confusion grew with each passing hour. In the middle of this chaos I could suddenly feel my stomach harden on me and the clenching that made me moan involuntarily: "Oh, Lord, please have mercy on me and don't let me deliver my baby now!" I cried. Not here, not in this dirty hay barn. I want my baby to live!" Again I felt the pinching and turning in my belly and then again and again. It scared me, but I didn't cry out in my distress. I had decided not to panic, come what may, neither would my shouting have helped. Oh, mother, help me, take my pain away. It was still about a month until the time of normal delivery, but in such circumstances anything could happen.

A new firing shattered the silence. I trembled. The unborn was kicking very hard and made me extremely uncomfortable. Breathlessly I stared into the darkness. I tried to think of Rolph at the front lines. Did he have time to think of me in this predicament? And my mother, if I only would have her beside me, everything would be easier. I thought of my lonesome life, somehow it didn't seem right, or fair.

In the darkness of the night my mind wandered back to the last days in Finland and to my stepfather. At a moment like this, I knew he was right when he told me I had nothing to offer my son, nothing but my love. Harri was better off where he was now than by my side in this forsaken hay barn. And yet, stepfather's harsh words haunted me, hurt me and ripped my heart to pieces, and I couldn't keep the tears from rolling down my cheeks. I felt like a bitter loser. I had changed from a vivacious young girl to a woman whose face was etched with the hardships and severity of my struggles to survive.

The din of the battle was slowly subsiding and so was the clenching and hardening of my belly. The good Lord was on my side. I didn't need to moan and groan any longer, and the kicking of the unborn had slowed down. No doubt the painful episode of labor pains had been just a pre-warning to what was now postponed. Was it God's hand guiding my way, or the spirit of my mother that helped me through?

Thankfully I turned to look at my sweet little angel by my side, she was fast asleep under the blanket of hay. I felt exhausted and tormented from all that strain, and fell in a restful and relaxed stupor, my face still wet from my tears.

As the first rays of the morning sun forced their way through the shrapnel torn roof of the barn and danced on the golden hair of my beloved Regine, I woke up and saw two of the most glorious blue eyes smiling at me and two softest little arms reaching out to caress me, and as she found my breast and lifted her head to eagerly suckle a few drops of my scarce milk, I knew I was a winner—she needed me and I needed her. I thanked the good Lord for her.

There was a death-like stillness around us. The sound of war was gone. It seemed like there were only two of us human beings in the whole wide world.

But in the far distance I could hear a rooster crowing to announce the start of a new day. We will make it, God willing.

By the middle of April 1945, American tanks began to appear. They were coming from all directions. A change was about to take place, and before long the American soldiers were forcing their way into all buildings and shacks, taking many men as prisoners. Paul was among them. We tried to hide him in the piles of hay, but they found him and took him along. I felt I had lost a real friend, and my last hope for help in the days ahead.

Soon white flags began to appear on the house tops and people began to climb out from their hiding places wearing white rags in their hands or tied around their sleeves as an indication of surrender. I too stepped out of the barn, took one of the diapers still hanging on the tree and tied it to my arm. The worst was over, and the life blood still flowed in me; although the future was still an uncertainty, at least death wasn't pressing at my heels.

We refugees welcomed the American army with tears of thankfulness.

A deep sigh rose from my throat. *I'll see my Rolph again, and he will be with me when our baby will be born. And someday we will have a home of our own.* I began to sing to my Regine again. Spring was here and I could hear the birds sing and twitter and sense the smell of earth, and I felt like being alive.

CHAPTER 32
Aftermath

The war was still going on. The front had merely moved back into the interior of the country.

The city of Bayreuth surrendered that same day, but some SS groups, flushed out of hiding, fought desperately.

It was the victorious American Army that liberated us from the terrors of the war. The people rejoiced and embraced each other in the streets. Still it seemed impossible to believe. It was almost too good to be true.

No more bombs disturbed our sleep. Airplanes were overhead, and though we would shrink instinctively, nothing would
happen, no bombs fell. It was wonderful.

Evacuees and refugees tried to find their way back to
their former homes, even those who knew they had lost them.

After a short wait, I, too, took to the road again, planning
to go back to Bayreuth. I was anxious to find a place to live
for the sake of Regine and the birth of my new baby. My body
seemed very heavy, and my feet were worn out and my back
hurt at every step. I was due to deliver in two weeks. Progress
was slow. The journey seemed endless. I begged some passersby to help me to push my carriage, but everyone seemed
so involved in their own endeavors and refused.

Arriving, finally, in the city, I found that the room where
I had lived, and where some of my belongings had been left,
had been taken over by the American army. The civilians in
the area were busily carrying away their possessions, for they
had been ordered to evacuate. I had arrived just in time to
rescue the few things I had left there.

I went into the house and asked an American soldier who
stood nearby for permission to go to the attic and get my
belongings. I had left Regine outside in the carriage, as I
planned to be gone but a minute. Soldiers stared curiously at
me, perhaps because I spoke a little English. One young
Ukrainian in American uniform told me to come and show
him where my stuff was.

Unsuspecting, I climbed the stairs with him. Stepping
into the room after me, he closed and locked the door and
put the key into his pocket. I was speechless with fright and
couldn't move. I just stared at him. He pushed me towards
the bed and took hold of me. Then only did my brain begin
to function. I shoved him frantically from me and screamed:
"Don't touch me. Kill me if you wish, but don't forget that

you'll have two murders on your conscience. I am expecting a baby."

"You are lying," the man said. "When are you supposed to have it?"

"In two weeks, if you don't mind." He was startled and just stood and stared at me, then let me go, watching me uncertainly. Once more he came closer, putting his hand on my stomach to be sure that I wasn't lying. I held my breath and arched my back to make up for my lack of size in the stomach. Then he went to the door, opened it and disappeared without a word. I couldn't get out of that house fast enough.

We were without shelter again. It was already evening, and I couldn't find anyone who could take us in. I stood on the side of the road long after civilians were supposed to be off the streets. Hard blasts of wind came whistling around the street corner, making me shiver. Soon an army patrol arrived and asked me sharply if I didn't realize that it was dangerous and forbidden to be on the street at that hour. Fearfully, I explained to them that I had no place to go. On hearing this, the soldiers motioned for me to follow them. We walked on and on until they finally stopped in front of a house, rang the bell, and told the woman who opened the door to take me and the baby in. She refused at first, but seeing that they were giving her little choice in the matter, she let us in, annoyance showing clearly on her face.

Hanna, the owner of the house, softened towards me after awhile and became friendly. I was dead tired, however, and after taking care of the baby, I soon fell asleep on the living room floor.

It must have been the middle of the night when I heard a loud rapping at the door. It scared us all, and Regine started crying. Hanna staggered to the door and opened it slightly. But the door flew open with one jerk, and in walked two soldiers in full uniform and gear. One of them gave Hanna a small can of real coffee and said "You cook coffee for us."

They started to unload their gear, placing it on the chairs, and then took out crackers and cookies, putting them on the table. Regine was given a piece of milk chocolate. She grabbed it and stuffed it into her mouth immediately and then gave a big smile to the donor.

When the coffee was ready, the soldiers, Amys as we called them, made us drink it first, before they even touched it to make sure it was safe. Our conversation was simple and brief, since Hanna didn't speak any English and I was too frightened to say much.

One of the soldiers finally pointed his finger at Hanna and said: "My friend will sleep with her," and pointing at me, "and I will sleep with you."

I was startled at first but quickly snatched my baby in my arms and stated flatly: "Don't touch me, I'm pregnant!" That had helped me once before.

"That won't bother us," said the soldier, "and it won't hurt you."

That was too much for me, and I ran crying with my baby in my arms out of the door and into the night.

After the soldiers finally got the message and left, I returned to the house and slept fitfully for the rest of the night.

The following day I borrowed a bicycle, and leaving my Regine with Hanna, I started out to get my sack of goods which I had hidden in the hay barn about five miles away. Can you imagine a woman about eight months pregnant pedaling a bicycle? It must have been a sight, but I did it!

The road was littered with military vehicles that were casualties of the war, making my progress slow. There was an unbearable stench from the bodies of victims still left in the field of battle, but I was determined to get through. As far as I could see, the road was sprinkled with returning refugees. Despair had disappeared from their face, and replacing it was a stolid resignation.

The sun shone brightly and warm and the air was fresh

171

and blessed on my face. Along the old battle fields were some wild flowers ready to bloom. Yellow, white and blue patches of them brightened the area where the war had left its tracks, and they brightened up my mind. The bicycle ride required a great deal of effort, and I was very thankful I made it. I found my sack and made all haste to get back to the city before curfew, but although I hurried as much as possible, I was too late. The city was closed to everyone for the night. Fresh army contingents were expected to pass through and no one was allowed on the roads leading into the city. Guards in full gear stood around shouting warning signals and pointing their guns at me. I had to think fast. Suddenly it came to me, and I motioned to a soldier who then walked over to me.

"I must get through to my baby," I said showing him my Finnish passport.

"She is only ten months old and is being watched by strangers. I must get home to nurse her!" I begged him.

"We are not allowed to let anyone pass," he shouted angrily. "It is very dangerous and you may get killed." Again he pointed the gun at me.

"I'll pedal fast through the fields. I am not afraid," I pleaded with him, "Please, please let me go through!"

After a long hesitation, he finally said: "Go ahead then, but hurry. You are at your own risk," and he motioned me to go.

I went pell-mell through the fields toward the city and could hear warning shouts and shots, but frantically pedaled on and on. Just as I reached the first rows of houses I saw a contingent of soldiers arriving. Luck had been with me this time.

When I came closer to the house where I had left Regine, I saw Hanna with my carriage disappear behind the corner. I panicked. Where could she be going with my child? I chased after her and finally caught her.

"Where are you going?" I asked.

"You came just in time. We've been evacuated from this area. The American army is taking over our buildings and we must leave," explained Hanna.

She handed the baby carriage over to me and Regine, recognizing me, lifted her little arms up to greet me. Thank heaven we were together again.

Hanna was in a hurry to leave and told me she was going to leave town to stay with her relatives. They wouldn't have room for me. I was dumbfounded, we were left on the streets again without shelter.

Now the painful, humiliating search for a room began once more. I rang a few doorbells, but without luck. Some people were kind, others downright rude and rejected us, flinging the door shut in front of me.

I sat down on some steps nearby. I was miserable, exhausted and terribly hungry. I hated begging others to help me. I wanted to be able to take care of myself and my children, but my hands were tied. I had no place to start. But as soon as I would hear from Rolph the outlook would change.

When I heard the sound of wheels coming up the walk I looked up, startled. Could it be a patrol, as this was the curfew time? But no, it wasn't. I saw a tall, middle-aged woman pushing the wheelchair of an older, white-haired lady.

"Do you wish to spend the night here?" she asked me.

I nodded unhappily, "I thought I might have to spend the night here on the steps."

"We have the keys to the upper apartment," the younger woman said. "We are staying for a few days until the owner returns. You may stay with us if you wish."

If I wished! I was relieved beyond description, and followed them up the steps. The old saying, "A friend in need is a friend indeed," is very true.

The younger woman, named Schwester Eugenie, a nurse, explained that the old, paralyzed lady in the wheelchair was her mother, the widow of the late counselor Seufferheld and that she was their daughter. Because they had lost their home in the raid a few days ago, they hoped to find a permanent house before long. I sat and listened while they talked of their experiences and prepared a meal for us.

Then we sat down to eat at a table covered with a white cloth. Can I ever forget that moment? I fingered the clean cloth and eyed every dish placed on the table. Then Frau Seufferheld said grace in German, and we ate.

As the first meal for us since the end of the war, they brought out steamed potatoes that were like apples of Hesperides and canned meat in honor of the occasion. To me this meal was better than any fancy cooking offered by a luxury restaurant. Regine was attended to as well and was given something to eat she had never had before: hot chocolate, apple butter, home-made bread. And we were able to make diapers for her out of old sheets to replace the rags and paper I had once been carrying with me. We devised some pants and jackets for her out of old clothing the lady had, and my baby looked like a pretty little doll smiling brightly as we put on her new clothes. She won everybody's heart.

One day we heard rumors that food depots established by the Germans had been raided and the doors were open. A mob of people were moving in from all directions to get a share of these treasures. Apparently the warehouses had been partly wrecked by bombs and some of the food was scattered about on the streets. This told us where the huge stocks were and the news spread like wild fire. When people approached the area, however the army patrols chased them away. But just as soon as the soldiers turned their backs, another group rushed into the warehouses. Not only food but also clothing had been stored in those barracks. It seemed wrong that those buildings had stood fully stocked with goods while people were starving. When I saw a crowd carrying bags of flour and meal, I decided to try my luck. But rather than take anything without permission, I decided to ask the patrols. As I approached the area I saw an armed soldier standing outside the warehouse and he didn't seem to care about the intruders. I decided to ask him, and I climbed over great heaps of rubble until I stood before him. I showed him my Finnish papers, which had helped me before, and told him of my needs. Another guard came over to question me also, and then together they walked ahead of me into the building and told me I could take whatever I wanted. How lucky I was!

I wished I had a truck to carry away a small fraction of what lay before my eyes! There were great piles of sacks, from floor to ceiling, containing flour, sugar, salt and coffee, as well as cereals. I watched as some people slashed open boxes and bags as well as cans to determine what was inside, and then walked away leaving foods to pour out onto the wet, dirty floors. And it wasn't as if they felt they had the right to do so. They would sneak around, as if pursued, and then glance from side to side before gathering all they could carry. Why was there so much waste? I wondered. I wanted to be careful not to waste one precious drop of anything, because I was thankful and happy to get food again.

There had been weeks when we hadn't had a bit of fat or butter and very little bread. Most of the grocery stores had been burned and the rest had been broken into and looted. We ate a lot of soup then, made out of a yellow powder that looked like sawdust. We called it gruel. This porridge was available at designated places with our ration cards. Now we had a respite from the great hunger that gnawed at us and we enjoyed those days tremendously. However, it ended soon. Supplies just weren't adequate in the city and were soon depleted.

I worried that I wasn't getting enough nutrition for the new baby. And what if I didn't have enough milk for nursing?

Could I keep the baby alive? I had to push my worries aside. But the unborn kept kicking and turning, constantly reminding me of my predicament. All I could do was wait, and hope that things would turn out all right. I trusted when Rolph would be back everything would be taken care of. We could go back to Finland and get my dear Harri. It would be heavenly! All of us, together again. I had faith in God!

Early in May the owners of the house returned and we were again without a place to stay. However, a new law was in force ruling that those buildings whose owners didn't return within a certain length of time, would be available as lodgings for others. So it happened that a missing SS officer's apartment near our street was given to us for lodgings. There were two small rooms and a kitchen. One of the rooms was so full of trunks and furniture that we couldn't use it, so the Seufferhelds used the bedroom and I slept on the kitchen sofa with Regine.

We had no dishes or cooking utensils, nor could they be bought for love or money. Then we heard of freight cars loaded with half-burned goods. Some friends had been getting their dishes from there. So it came that Schwester Eugenie and I, both carrying large bags, set out in search of kitchen utensils. We knew that it was probably dangerous and that we risked being beaten up by others who claimed the whole trainload for themselves. Now and then fights had broken out between Polish D. P.'s (displaced persons) and Germans. But we ventured there.

What a relief! There were only two small boys who hurriedly gathered dishes in their sacks. Being the younger, I climbed into one of the cars. Once safely in, I began a search. It wasn't very easy to find unbroken plates and cups among the piles of broken goods. The pieces scratched and cut my hands as I moved about. But every whole plate and cup I found I handed down to Schwester Eugenie, and it was tucked safely into our bags.

We had collected a number of the more important pieces we needed when we heard one of the boys cry out: "Run! Run! They're coming!" I looked out and saw men heading our way with long cat-o-nine-tails (a kind of whip) in their hands.

The boys jumped down as quickly as squirrels and ran off. I, as rapidly as I could in my condition, jumped off the car too, and we ran over rocks and stumps dragging our bags after us. Some of the dishes broke, but at least we saved our skins. I felt like a schoolgirl running away after stealing apples.

We had lived in our room only a few days when an army patrol went from house to house announcing that the whole street had to be evacuated in an hour. The American army was going to occupy the houses. Once more we despaired at the thought of being homeless. Frau Seufferheld, who was eighty-five years old, couldn't be comforted. She cried continually. "What crime have I committed, that I should be thus punished? First my home destroyed, then my husband killed, and now I'm driven from house to house. There is no peace for me in my old age."

Then I decided to try to do something. I took my Finnish pass, and went to see the commander of the battalion. After much difficulty, I was able to talk to the captain who was busily quartering his men in the first empty houses. I explained my business and showed my pass, but he only shook his head and said: "What do you want me to do? I can't make any exceptions and leave civilians in the buildings." I begged and pleaded with him to let us have at least one room since we were refugees and had nowhere to go. I explained that we had a paralyzed lady with us who needed help and care. Finally the captain agreed to let us use two rooms. However, he went with me to investigate and make sure I was telling the truth. Finally he posted a warning on our door: "KEEP OUT." When I returned with the good news, I found Schwester Eugenie had packed all our belongings and was all ready to leave. She couldn't believe what good fortune had come our way. But when I convinced her, she gladly carried everything back and put it in its place. We had a home for the time being.

CHAPTER 33
The Waiting Ends

On May 8, 1945, Germany accepted the terms of peace. On that day a great sigh of relief could be heard around the world. Though life wouldn't become easier for a long time to come, at least the fighting was over.

Gang wars, robberies and even murder became everyday occurences, however. It seemed that all who thought they had been wronged by the German government now wanted their revenge. And many found opportunities for wreaking vengeance. The police, as well as other organizations that offered protection, had been disbanded when the Nazi regime fell, and no new system for civilian control or defense had been set up. Gangs formed, and unsuspecting civilians were robbed of clothes, money, and jewelry. Many of the gangs were made up of displaced persons, "DP's," who wandered about idly, getting their daily rations from the UN organization that was there to provide aid.

The displaced persons in Germany were a large and mixed lot. One could see not only Russians and Poles, but also Czecho-Slovaks, Swedes, Danes, Ukrainians, Estonians and many more. American occupation authorities tried sending many back to their own countries. Truckloads of them were brought to the borders of their nations, but before long they trickled back into the big cities where aid and rations were more easily available.

People had to have identification. Many wore a small flag to distinguish themselves from the Germans. I made a tiny Finnish flag out of scraps of blue and white cloth and fastened it on my coat. I thought of the blue as a symbol of Finland's blue skies, and the white as a symbol of the abundant snows that cover the land. That flag proved to be of great help on many occasions.

Food was still a problem and seemed to get worse each day even after the war had ended. Inflation was on its way, and money, if one had any, was almost worthless. Frau Seufferheld's husband had died leaving a pension to support his widow for the rest of her life. She used this pension until the war was almost ended. Then there was no organization to manage the funds and she lost her income, living on her savings hidden at home.

In spite of these hardships I found the Frau, Oma, as we called her, and Schwester Eugenie ready to do everything possible to help me and my baby. One by one they sold their antiques and keepsakes to the highest bidder to keep food on the table, and not once did I feel that they saw me as a burden. The loss of personal belongings and keepsakes was sad for us all, but I'll never forget the bitter tears Oma shed when she parted with her husband's pocket watch. It was difficult to have to stand by and not be able to do anything to alleviate the suffering.

The summer brought a lot of rain. The days were dark, stormy and damp. With Regine in my lap I sat and listened for hours to the endless pounding of the rain on our window. It looked like a never ending chain of beads. We couldn't do much while it rained, and we were anxious to begin a search of Oma's destroyed home for useable articles, but when the rain finally ceased, it was time to begin. Part of the building was still standing and this made it even more dangerous, but we proceeded to sift through. Sometimes Schwester Eugenie stood lost in her thoughts in the midst of the ruins of her former home. Tears ran down her cheeks as she moved the black ashes with her foot. This had once been a home, a place of security for her. All was in ashes. A corner of her grand piano stuck out from the rubble, and a portrait, which looked like one of her father, still hung crookedly on the one remaining wall, badly battered. Our search provided nothing but pain. We didn't go back again.

On a gloomy Saturday morning in the middle of May, I received a small, printed card telling me that Rolph was reported dead. Like thousands of others, he was missing in action, final fate unknown. I was dumbfounded. Premonitions had forewarned me and a strange feeling often had plunged me into deeper gloom. But I had been hoping, and until the last moment, a germ of hope had stayed in my heart. Now it was definite! I would never see my beloved Rolph again.

Gone were our dreams of a home in Finland. Gone was our happiness and love. Never, never again would I awake to a bright, sunny day. Had God deserted me? All my numbed brain could say was: Why? Why? There are no words to describe this tragedy.

That night I bathed in my tears. My life seemed of such little consequence, and I didn't see anything beautiful and lovely in this world.

In the dark of the night my thoughts went back to my fatherland. Over and over again I was asking myself why I had left Finland.

Was it because of the painful, tattered past that was pressuring me, or was it the hopefully rosy future with a man I loved that lured me? I found no answer!

So many, many times I had wished I could go back and start all over again, and now, after the message of Rolph's death, the thought came back very strongly: I was tired of living. If I only could fall asleep—a long, long sleep and wake up in the spring when the whole world would be in bloom—and feel keenly alive—find a path and run through fields of flowers in thrilling colors—and find myself in Finland . . . by my son.

When the first rays of the sun peeked in through my window, a sudden little babbling noise beside me woke me up and I was looking at two gorgeous, smiling blue eyes. In a sudden urge, I grabbed my little Regine in my arms, and as I felt her warm body against mine, I knew all the answers I needed to know: I had something to live for—something that was worth more than gold—I had something that needed me.

Would I ever leave her?
Never—she was mine!
Dear God, give me strength.

There was a search organization that operated in all parts of the country, which tried to trace members of families and help them get together again. I wrote to this organization hoping to get further information of Rolph's fate, or his parents whereabouts, but I heard nothing. In vain I listened to the radio for news of refugees, but it was futile. Now I knew that my baby would be born with no Dad to welcome her. That was my fate.

But my sorrow had no end!

I gazed into another world, and my thoughts kept going over and over the unforgettable experiences which I could never comprehend. The memories were too many and the past too close, but I said to myself: I can't stop living now!

CHAPTER 34
A Brush with a Russian Soldier

It was June, the month of my new baby's birth. Hunting for food was still a daily chore. Things had become progressively more and more difficult, and there were no organizations to even begin to take care of all the people's needs. One day I went to trace the rumor that one could get canned meat from an ex-military storage. It turned out to be a very hazardous outing.

I approached the warehouse where the canned food was said to be, and looked for a guard. There were several men standing in a group, an American, a Russian and some others of varying nationalities. I didn't feel comfortable being around these defenders. I feared that I might become a victim of their vengeful ire. I had heard about incidents whereby military men of different countries were wreaking vengeance on those who were identified as Germans. There were beatings, robberies, and plenty of verbal abuse.

Advancing toward an American soldier, I waved my I.D. papers in my hands. He noticed me and approached alone. I was rather afraid that one of the Russians might accompany him, and I had a deep-seated fear of them. But the American soldier read my papers and took me down to the basement, and then left me alone. I found there a huge mountain of boxes and crates and wished I could carry out as much as a mule.

I couldn't even begin to pick up one of the cases but did manage with a few cans. Just as I was ready to start home, I received such a kick in the back that I fell down onto the wet, muddy floor, and the cans scattered every which way. Looking up I found one of the Russian soldiers glowering down at me. I had seen him outside. "You damn Kraut, you out!" he was cursing. I staggered up on my feet and tried to explain that

I was a Finn, not a "Kraut," pointing to my papers, but he didn't seem to understand, or if he did, he didn't care. Roughly he took hold of my arm and pushed me out through the door. Luckily there were other soldiers around who came over and prevented any further abuse on his part. I was thankful there were such people as the American soldiers. They had showed more sympathy than I had thought possible, and they were friendly in contrast to the Russians, who stood out in my mind as excessively violent.

Two weeks after the report of Rolph's death, I received a letter from my good friend Elsa. She had been a close friend during my days in the opera. In fact, on the day before my flight from Poznan, she had come to me and asked me to flee with her. I only frowned at her then, and said I thought it unnecessary to panic. Now, many months later, the letter arrived from Flensburg, Northern Germany, asking me to come with Regine and live in her home. Elsa had tried unsuccessfully to trace me and finally secured my address from the newly established refugee organization. In her letter she stated that she was willing to help me during my coming confinement. What a surprising offer! Was help finally coming my way? I was excited about her generosity and did make a few inquiries about possible transportation. As it turned out, however, all transportation in Germany was disrupted, with bridges blown up and many stations in ruins. Automobile and bus service was also out of the question since there wasn't any fuel to keep them running. The only vehicles you could see on the roads were the American army convoys and a few military trucks. How wonderful it would have been to be able to go to my friend, but in my ready-to-deliver condition, it was unthinkable. I was downhearted, but at least I knew a friend was thinking of me and cared.

One day a visitor came to see me from the British occupation zone in Northern Germany. I was overjoyed to see our old friend Wowa standing before me. My girlfriend Paivi had asked him to search for me while on his way to Munich on a military excursion. Through Wowa I learned about Paivi's movements since we parted in Poznan. She had fled with her family to Germany, which later became the British occupation zone. Her husband was able to get employment at the University in Goettingen, and she had also finally found a teaching position there. I felt a strong bond between Paivi and me. Finns do stick together also when away from their homeland. Though I always hoped to see Paivi again, I never did get that chance. I had heard nothing of my in-laws since we parted in Baruth. After numerous inquiries I was told that they had been taken prisoner by the Russian. However, months later I found out they were living in an old peoples' home in Northern Germany. They had escaped to that zone by some stroke of luck and remained there unable to withstand further travel.

I hoped those dear relatives of mine would have a brighter old age, but I wasn't in a position to help them. I did make an effort to have them transferred to Bayreuth, in the American zone, later on. However, they were not well enough to travel and preferred staying where they were, hoping that someday I could come and live with them. That chance never came.

My beloved in-laws spent the rest of their days in the old peoples' home. Thus ended the days of the once brave and lovable man who lost his entire property three times through wars not of his making.

All he asked of the world was a chance to live a quiet and decent life.

From the time that we moved into the house among the soldiers on Kant Street, Schwester Eugenie and I had been going around in search of a hospital where I could stay with Regine while in confinement after the birth of my second baby. At first I had tried to get into a large private women's clinic which was situated on a high hill on the outskirts of the city. I set out to make inquiries there.

It was a most beautiful June day when we began the outing on foot. The snow had melted and green grass could be seen for the first time, nudging its way out between fallen stones, boards and bricks, and spreading its way out into the empty lots and fields. The road we were taking took us through much of the city's bombed-out section. There was a putrid smell of decay as the sun thawed the remains of people and dead animals among the ruins. Swarms of flies could be seen buzzing around these now rotting pieces of flesh.

We walked with our handkerchiefs to our noses, trying to get by before the stench made us too sick. We knew that germs were spreading rapidly in that area and already many people had fallen sick with diseases. Drinking water there was highly contaminated and typhus was making the rounds of those who didn't boil their water and cook foods properly.

At the hospital we had to wait for what seemed like hours before we saw a doctor. He arrived finally, and examined me carefully, advising me to come back in two weeks for my confinement. They were sorry to inform me, however, that Regine would not be allowed with me in the hospital. I would have to find another place for her.

I knew I couldn't stay at home. I was still without a proper bed and had to sleep on the couch in the kitchen. In addition, water was not readily available since we had to share with others in the neighborhood and stand in line for our turn to pump water from the nearest well. So, knowing that I would receive proper care at this hospital, I left feeling positive, hoping that I could find someone to take care of Regine while I was away.

But two days after our call at the hospital, I received a card informing me that the hospital was to be converted into an army installation and I would have to find other arrangements for my delivery. Immediately I went to the city general hospital to get advice, but unfortunately this hospital took only emergency cases and had no maternity ward. There remained only a Catholic convent hospital about six miles outside the city and we, Schwester Eugenie and I, hurried there on foot the following day.

We walked up and down steep hills and grenade-shredded woods. A slight breeze had come from the East to take the edge off the afternoon heat. The breeze felt good on my perspiring face, but when we finally arrived at our destination, I was thoroughly exhausted and sat down on a bench in the park to recuperate. I watched some small children playing in the yard, and I felt sure this would be an ideal place for me.

When we ventured inside the hospital, I was interviewed most thoroughly and given a physical examination. The Mother-Superior was very good to me, and I felt such relief to be under the care of competent personnel. I felt I could actually look forward to the delivery and cast off all my worries.

Luck was not with me this time either, however, when shortly after our visit to the hospital I learned there would be no more civilians admitted to the Catholic hospital unless it was an emergency. Thus my hopes for a normal, comfortable delivery of this baby were quickly dashed. I knew now, I would have to rely on a midwife, if available, and plan to have my child at home. It had all been a useless search.

On the evening of June 19, I was out for my usual evening

186

walk in the fields in back of our house while Regine was asleep. I thought I would pick a few wild flowers for Oma, for she loved them so much. The soft summer wind was like a balm for my tense body, and there was a delicious fragrance in the air. I breathed it in and watched the last rays of the sun disappear behind the woods. It was like a calm before the storm.

I was very restless and lonesome for Rolph to comfort me that night, and I felt slightly bitter in my predicament. I hadn't slept for several nights and was exhausted but couldn't sleep and wandered around in our cubby hole of a room gazing out of the window into the dark night. I softly stroked the little crib where my Regine lay, fast asleep, looking so sweet and innocent like a little angel. Her little white fists, plump and relaxed were so delicate against the rough, old, army blanket borrowed from a neighbor, which she was wrapped in. The sight and scent of her touched me, she was my pride and joy. I loved her so.

From time to time I could feel my stomach harden and the baby was kicking very strongly. I knew from my previous experience it wouldn't be long before the contractions would start. It was only eleven months ago when I had gone through this with Regine but then I had been at the hospital with all the help and care. I had made up my mind not to panic, though.

The night was endless. Here it was, the same hardening of the stomach and then clenching that made me crouch down and moan. This was for real, and the contractions were serious ones. I started pacing the floor like a lioness in her den, but I wasn't scared.

My feet were cold and I had no slippers so I sat down on the bed and pulled the blanket arond me. There I was all alone in a strange house, strange bed, and in Oma's old pink flannel nightgown, restlessly tossing and turning.

Suddenly I felt the coils of pain squeezing out of my tummy and encircling my whole body. Oh, Lord, give me strength! I must survive for my children.

I glanced at my little angel in her crib, she was still fast asleep. What would happen if anything would go wrong? Quickly I chased those thoughts away; I wanted to be strong.

The contractions were closer apart now and I knocked on the door to tell the news to the Seufferhelds, as planned.

Oma burst out crying and moaned: "Vikki, you poor child, where can we find help?"

I tried to calm her, assuring her that I would be all right, but in reality I was bewildered and didn't know for sure what was going to happen. Schwester Eugenie, although a trained nurse, informed me that she would not feel comfortable taking the responsibility for the birth and she left at once on foot to summon the midwife two miles way. But while she was gone my little dark-haired girl was born and I managed most of it myself. I was lucky that the afterbirth was normal and came without trouble.

The midwife, immediately upon her arrival, bathed and weighed the infant and I could hardly believe it when she told me that the baby weighed nine pounds. Nine pounds—in spite of the terrible conditions under which we had lived. Thank goodness she was alive and healthy.

I lay on the narrow couch-bed holding one baby on each side. On the table beside me were the flowers I had picked for Oma on the previous day. Now she had given them back to me for the occasion.

My children were truly all I had in the world, the two little angels by my side and Harri in Finland. They all needed love and care. How happy I would have been in other circumstances, and how proudly I would have shown the new baby to Rolph. Oh, Rolph, look down on your family. We need you so! All I had to offer those two half-orphans were my two empty hands, but the knowledge that they needed me gave me strength. I wanted to make a better life for them.

CHAPTER 36
Double Christening

The American soldiers had set up a field kitchen in our yard. Huge kettles of food cooked there all day long and wonderful odors drifted in through the windows. The soldiers had strict orders not to give food to civilians who were often hanging about. Children, thin and pale, were gathering in little flocks around the cooking area, grabbing discarded cans in the hopes of finding a little food left in them. They searched for partly spoiled fruit which the cooks had thrown away. Every garbage pile was searched, and it was no wonder that all kinds of diseases raged. Sometimes we were recipients of one friendly soldier's gifts of coffee or pancake flour. These getures of kindness we appreciated very much and we made a party out of the goodies he gave. Every little thing counted for a lot in those lean days.

One day I looked in the mirror and a strange face looked back at me. Who was this woman with the cynical mouth, the bitter, brooding eyes and the look of a desperately cornered animal? Could these few months have changed me so completely? The fights for survival had taken me through the sleet and cold of the elements, through fire and death of war, through starvation and illness and flights and fights to preserve my body from violation; oh, God—so much life had been lived in such a short time. Was I marked for life with this strange new countenance? I'm sure I didn't feel all the hatred I showed. It frightened me and I was glad my mother didn't see me like this. Dear God, let me find a way to restore my faith and my courage!

Then came that momentous evening in our little kitchen apartment. We all sat around our only lamp reading and chatting. I glanced at Regine, asleep in her carriage in the corner

189

of the room and Christel in her basket looking like a shriveled little doll, but sleeping quietly. Thank God I had been able to nurse her.

Suddenly there was a knock on the door and someone stood in the doorway glancing uncertainly at each of us. We were shocked! It was a tall soldier in U.S. uniform and full gear who stepped in and looked at us.

We are going to be ousted, I thought.

But his sober face changed to a broad grin and I heard: "No, hyvaa paivaa!" (Well, good day to you).

We were a bit startled and glanced wonderingly at each other. Hearing those familiar words in my mother tongue left me speechless. And before I could say anything he continued, nodding his head in my direction: "Are you the Finn?"

Only then did I come to my senses and get up to greet the visitor: "Yes, I am a Finn. Are you?"

"I'm a Finnish-American. Norman, is the name," he answered. "My father immigrated to America from Finland at the age of sixteen. I was born in Michigan."

"Norman," (I had never heard that name before), "How did you find me?" I continued.

The soldier, a very tall and friendly, blond nordic type, answered by saying that one of the cooks had mentioned that a girl wearing a Finnish flag on her coat was living in this building and he had decided to investigate.

As he talked the door opened and another soldier in full gear walked in. His name was Uuno and he was short and sturdy and also a Finn in the American army. He had come to our house at Norman's urging. I hadn't met any Finns since my friend Paivi in Poland, and it was all the more exciting to be able to converse in my native tongue again and share some experiences with these new-found friends. I felt that my home-land had moved closer. I welcomed the visitors gladly and we became closer and closer friends as time went on. And although

190

the ladies in my apartment couldn't understand a word of our conversation, they welcomed the soldiers warmly.

A somewhat brighter period followed for us. Whenever and wherever possible, Norman and Uuno were ready to help. They brought us everything they could lay their hands on. A big portion of their weekly rations found its way to our table in spite of the no fraternization rules for the soldiers.

Uuno had been a ship's electrician and had visited many countries and told many interesting stories. Norman was much quieter and a more serious man. He talked less and listened more. He quickly took to Regine and at each visit he brought all the chocolate he could carry in his pockets for her. Every time he stepped into the room Regine's little arms reached up for him. The big man and the little child made a touching picture together.

I grew to look forward to Norman's visits and so did Regine. We truly appreciated his kindness, warmth and his help. I found myself feeling more like a human being again, now that we had friends who cared.

I decided to baptize both children on Regine's first birthday in July. She had not been baptized for the simple reason that I had waited for her father to be present and no opportunity showed itself. Now the ladies and I decided a double christening would be appropriate. Oma and Schwester Eugenie were to be witnesses.

For the christening we fixed up the other bedroom which, until now, was full of furniture and trunks. We carried all the trunks and boxes out into the shed and soon the room was ready. In the middle of the floor a large table and chairs took up half of the space. We lifted one cupboard up onto another to make room for the baby carriage which still served as Regine's bed. (That blessed carriage was a life saver!).

Now there was just enough room for the wash basket in which the new infant Christel slept. Norman was a great help to us during this operation as we couldn't move the heavy furniture alone. A long davenport under the window became my bed. Oma's freshly washed and ironed curtains on the window, and our room was in parade order for the christening.

Norman and Uuno wangled some white flour and other baking needs out of the army cook. They also liberated a few eggs from somewhere, and we made some delicious christening cakes such as we had not seen in over a year. In addition, our soldier friends brought us real coffee, which topped the delicacies.

Everything was arranged: the minister, the midwife (who is very important in a christening ceremony in Germany) godparents, and guests. There were not many of the latter, to be sure, for who could afford a large gathering. Nor were there any relatives, but we were satisfied with our little group of friends. As at so many other sentimental moments in my life, I thought of my mother and wished she could have been there with us, it would have meant so much to me to share my children's lives with her.

A good neighbor had made each of my girls a little dress from old white curtains, and there were tiny wreaths made of flowers to go on their heads. The girls looked delicate and lovely.

The great day arrived and all went smoothly except for a small snag in our plans. My friends, Rudy and Rita who were to have acted as godparents at the ceremony sent word that they couldn't be present. Since they were the only couple who had a car we were counting on their promise to take us all to the church. Now that was out. Where could I get godparents at the last moment? We were about to postpone everything but the mid-wife came upon the scene and insisted that nothing should stop us now, the pastor was waiting at the church and we could get our soldier friends to act as witnesses. She then set into motion our plan by dressing the girls to go while we hastily hunted up Norman and Uuno, asking them to be our emergency godparents. They consented with pleasure and we were all ready to go.

An old white church in the center of the city was chosen for the baptism. All of its windows were broken by the bombings, but it did not spoil our festive mood.

We walked to the church and the way was long. Poor Oma had to stay home. We arrived just as the morning services were ending and the baptism took place at once.

The midwife took each baby to the altar (as was the custom in Germany), then she gives it to the godfather to hold for the rest of the ceremony. This was Norman's duty. And finally the mother takes the child and is blessed with it. I held Regine first and then the little one. The ceremony was solemn and impressive.

Those two American soldiers in their uniforms at the altar, each with a baby in his arms were symbols of the war and humanity in all their contradictions. I couldn't keep back the tears as I contemplated our situation and felt the waves of gratitude wash over me. It brought home to me the fact that my babies were fatherless and that I would have a big job ahead of me. Would I be able to bring them up as proper members of a Christian congregation?

But the sun spilled its splendor on the many pieces of the broken windows, and the altar before me was in its glorious path. It kindled a spark of new hope in my soul—a small hope that I could succeed, if I lived, and God willed.

Our little party was jolly and gay that day, and we forgot our miseries of the past and the hard days ahead.

The church record in Bayreuth added the names Regine Solveig Talvikki and Christel Kirsten Sinikka, and I felt I had accomplished something important and was starting out well in a new phase of my life.

Five weeks after the birth of little Christel I became ill with pneumonia. My biggest concern was the care of the children. I couldn't ask Schweter Eugenie for she had started working at a hospital again and Oma was not capable of taking care of them since she was unable to walk. Norman and Uuno had given the children a sum of money as a gift, and I used that for payment to a young girl who came in to help me for a short while. But the money didn't last long, and I was forced to get back on my feet before I had fully recovered. Thank God my little Christel was getting along fine at the moment.

When finances were tight again and food was our primary concern, I was forced to reach into my bundle of family treasures and pull out a five-stone emerald ring which I would have to sell. I remember clearly how that ring had adorned my mother's slender finger. It was a treasure I hated to part with more than any other. I was about to part with the last physical tie with my mother, but I was not in a position to hesitate. I put the ring into my pocket and set out to make a trade. It broke my heart.

With money from the ring we were able to buy foods for a while again. But I knew I would have to go to work soon to bring in money regularly. I began by making some inquiries and learned that jobs were almost nil. There were so few factories that had survived the bombings and so few merchants who could afford help. Schools had not been reorganized yet, and I suppose my language deficiency might have prevented me from getting a teaching job there. I lacked any confidence and had a great many doubts about what I could be hired to do. I continued to keep my ear open for news about employment, however, for I knew I couldn't give up.

Meanwhile, our neighborhood had become a regular

home away from home for the American soldier. They had settled in and virtually taken over the area for themselves. In fact, many times we were even serenaded by a powerful loud speaker which had been placed high in a tree across the street from us, as record after record played, and soldiers sat around on time off, singing and whistling the familiar tunes. "You Are My Sunshine" and "Good, Good, Good" were popular songs at that time. These were strange and wonderful new sounds the Americans were introducing to the natives.

Regine seemed to enjoy the loud music, for she would sit in her carriage or on the floor and rock back and forth. She had had so little opportunity for such stimulation up until then. For quite some time the Germans had forbidden any sort of dance music to be played on the radio, and there was very little to choose from.

Oma didn't understand such modern racket and complained that it bothered her ears. When she heard something like "Pistol Packing Mama" she motioned for the windows to be closed and shook her head unhappily.

One day a group of us friends, Rita, Rudy, Norman and I made plans to take a short trip into the country to hunt for mushrooms for a feast in honor of Uuno, who was leaving Europe soon. He was assigned to the Pacific Theater of Military Operations. We had good weather that day, and we walked merrily across open fields and through woods, selecting all the edible mushrooms for our basket. I enjoyed being in Nature's shrine, with the dark green spruce forming the walls, the moss as its floor and the blue sky as its roof. I felt at home here in the woods as I had so many years before in Finland. Norman found me there, and together we enjoyed the peace and beauty of nature. He seemed to understand how much it all meant to me, and our mutual feelings of appreciation didn't require any words.

A sudden thunderstorm surprised us just as we were

getting ready to go home and we got a thorough drenching. But we had achieved what we set out to do, that is, gather a dinner's worth of tasty mushrooms, and so we didn't really care. Let it rain.

After our dinner we found Uuno, who had become quite inebriated. Norman had a difficult time escorting him out of the house. There was an eleven o'clock curfew and there was no time to lose. After Uuno reached the street he stood below our window and began emptying his pockets, describing each article as he placed it on the wall beside him. "Wallet, cigarettes, matches, hanky, chewing gum, keys, penicillin, fingernail cutters, and goddamned shit paper," he called out loud like an auctioneer.

But that wasn't all. He found one more item in his pocket which he proudly lifted high up in the air and exclaimed: "Aha, I found you, you little rascals! Goodbye, lovers, I don't need you anymore!"

The sight was sadly comical and attracted so much attention that a crowd gathered around him, enjoying the show, and laughing at every drunken ... e. It was hilarious, but it was also a sad farewell, and Uun. perhaps couldn't express it in any other way. That was the last we ever saw of him.

It wasn't long before Norman left. He was transferred from Bayreuth to Regensburg and that meant more than a hundred miles away. He had been a true friend, trying his best to keep my mind from dwelling on the dismal past. We were as close as any brother and sister.

While Uuno and Norman had been around they had tried to provide me with some medicines as well as foodstuffs. Christel had not looked well for quite some time, and we were all worried about her. Her yellow and pinched face wasn't healthy. Anyone knew by just looking at her that she was not well, and my heart was gripped with uncertainty and fear as I watched her in her restless sleep. She looked so pale and sick. I really didn't know if she would live or die. A doctor suggested some medicines but the major factor contributing to her ill health seemed to be poor nutrition. That was a problem not easy to solve. I had run out of breast milk quite early due to my own poor health and the only milk available to anyone was powdered milk. She was too young for solids, so I couldn't supplement the milk. I tried everything suggested and then waited and worried.

One evening I heard an automobile in front of the house. Then there were heavy footsteps on the stairs. I opened the door and there stood a very tall man dressed in a long, hooded raincoat, carrying a big rucksack on his back. It was Norman. He had come to see us on a few days' leave and was shocked at my thinness and my serious face, but decided he would cheer me up while he was there.

When Norman opened his sack I saw can after can of goodies come tumbling out onto the table. Meat, fruit, butter, cheese, and coffee. And chocolate for Regine. We had a big celebration. He stayed with us for two days, and when he left he promised he would be back at Christmas. After he left I found an envelope on the table addressed to "My Godchild Regine." The envelope contained a sum of money. What a friend! He did so much for us.

As I got stronger day by day, Christel seemed to get worse. Among other things she was suffering from a skin ailment caused by malnutrition. According to the doctor, oil massage would be a help. But oil was difficult to get. I had to trade my fat ration for oil, and with this I prepared an ointment. It wasn't nearly enough but I was thankful I had even a little. There were a number of successive ailments that Christel suffered, but little by little we saw her improve. Our friend Dr. Angerers made every attempt to help out and offered medicines from his meager supplies. I always felt grateful to him for helping Christel to pull through.

A few days before Christmas I received a short letter from Norman containing the news that he would be arriving on Christmas Eve. It was good news to all of us and we began to set in a festive mood. Oma and Schwester Eugenie and I talked of food preparations and gifts and set to work to create a happy holiday. I made a pullover for Norman from unraveled yarn from an old sweater. I wove into it a scene of deer in the snow, which were to me a symbol of the peace and beauty of nature that we both loved. For the children, garments were made from old pieces of cloth.

On Christmas Eve morning we heard a loud toot right under our window. Looking out we saw Norman with a jeep that carried big white letters spelling Vikki on its side. I was touched by his sentimentality and thrilled to see our friend again. He had been traveling since the night before. He wanted to have time to get a Christmas tree with me. Of course, he carried a big sack which I guessed would be full of Christmas goodies.

That afternoon we went looking for a Christmas tree. We drove out into the country in his jeep. It had been snowing lightly and the branches of the trees were dusted. The snow crackled under our feet and the frost nipped our cheeks to a rosy red. It was good to be alive. Nature seemed to revive me.

Norman had received a package from his home in America containing Christmas ornaments. We trimmed the tree with great care and placed it on the table. Then he put his small, colorful packages around it while I glanced curiously at them, wondering what was hiding inside.

I wanted to give the children a gift toy but could not consider buying one. Norman made a suggestion that turned out to be ingenious and offered hours of delight for the girls and us. We obtained a piece of used white oilcloth from Oma, on which I drew a picture of an elephant. We then cut it out piece by piece and then sewed the various pieces together by hand, using heavy red yarn. We couldn't agree on which way the elephant's ears should face and finally had to compromise by placing one ear forward and one backward. The animal was filled with balls of paper, and the stitching completed, we had a masterpiece. It was a fine, big animal and proved to be Regine's favorite toy. She could hardly carry it, but it was the very first present the eighteen-month-old child ever had.

After a simple but pleasurable meal, we sat around enjoying our tree and opening the few packages. The girls enjoyed the rattling of the colorful paper from America and it delighted us all. What a good friend I had in Norman. At a time when I had seen so little of human kindness and sharing, he came into my life. I was feeling more hope and faith in our future, and I was sure it was in great part due to Norman's efforts. It had been a very gloomy world for me, but it was beginning to brighten. In the quiet night I heard a soft melody: "Thus spoke a heavenly angel . . ."

CHAPTER 38
A Breadwinner Again

Right after Christmas I went to the employment office to meet Mr. Jansen, who I had heard was looking for English-speaking personnel for the American Army. There was a long wait before I was finally able to see him.

"What do you want?" said a grouchy voice when I entered the room. I saw a middle-aged man, wearing a sour face, sitting behind the desk. My chances for employment suddenly seemed mighty slim.

"I'm looking for work, and I speak English," I said timidly.

"What can you do?" he asked, now turning towards me.

Then followed a lengthy explanation about my schooling

and my former positions. He suddenly seemed more at ease, changed from speaking German to English and began telling me about his own experiences as a refugee, from Latvia.

When we parted, we were like old friends and he said, "You are a brave girl. I will do all I can for you." Not many days after my visit a notice of a job interview came to my home. The American Red Cross was looking for a hostess for their hospital, and I had been recommended by Mr. Jansen.

I went at the appointed time to see the superintendent. I borrowed an old but good-looking suit and a pair of shoes from Schwester Eugenie. I wanted to look neat. When I was interviewed, however, I felt uncomfortable while facing the cold and overly-formal superintendent in uniform, and when she asked me where my husband was, I cringed.

"He's dead, Ma'am," I replied.

"Was he a Finn, too?"

"No, an Estonian. He was studying in Finland and then we came to Germany where he finished his studies and was drafted into the Wehrmacht."

"Wehrmacht," she repeated, and then looking as if she had just seen an enemy in front of her, she sat up stiffly and said, "The interview is over. The position is no longer open, I'm sorry." She wrote "not accepted" on a piece of paper and shoved it at me. Close to tears, I took it and left feeling as if I had been branded.

I returned to Mr. Jansen's office to tell him what had happened. He was so certain I would be hired that he was very surprised. He suggested that I could have lied about some of the things in my past, but I never imagined that this would be the way to get a job. I vowed to be more cautious, at least, the next time.

New Year's Eve arrived. I returned home exhausted from a few hours of food foraging and found Norman playing with the children. He had come as a surprise, to spend New Year's with us. I was so pleased to see his happy face, a face that didn't carry the deep lines and furrows of worry and fear that I could see on so many faces around me.

There was a concert planned at the Wagner Opera House and Norman invited me to go. For the first time during my stay in Bayreuth I would be able to hear and see something light and gay. I had longed for good music but hadn't heard any, nor was I able to practice during those months.

It was nearly a three-mile walk to the opera house, but we arrived there full of expectations only to find the building dark and deserted looking. The doors were locked and a note was barely discernable on the door: "The concert is postponed."

The year 1946 began in gloom, with no end in sight. Poverty and hunger still threatened us all. People were committing suicide due to their hopeless situations. Although vaccinations were offered in all parts of the city and serums were given out by the U.S. army for all those who had been exposed to typhoid fever and other diseases, the contagions spread. More and more quarantine notices could be seen in the neighborhoods.

To my sorrow, Christel, who had never been very strong, was stricken with a virus. It was difficult to watch her suffering and to not be able to help her. Again all I could do was to watch her carefully and wait—and hope and pray.

It was a very cold winter again. We wore our coats in the house and many people preferred staying in bed in order to keep warm, or walking the streets to keep the blood circulating. Poor Oma suffered very much since the rooms were damp, the walls were mildewed and the clothes were cold and musty.

Oma also fell ill with the flu and lay many weeks in bed. We thought her end had come. We took the children in to see her in the evenings before they were put to bed, lifting them to the edge of her bed where they kneeled while Oma read an evening prayer. The wrinkled old face would lighten up a little, though, when she felt their tiny arms around her neck. "Oma's little sweethearts," she called them. Her interest in them may have been what kept her going so long.

In the middle of January Norman came again for a visit. He told me then that he would be leaving for the U.S. soon and wanted to try to help me all he could before he left.

"Vikki, I hate to leave you with that bitter look on your pretty face. I want to help you to stop looking back, just look ahead. Tomorrow brings another chance for happiness."

"It's easy for you, Norman. You have a country, and a home. And you have a future to look forward to. I don't know where to start." I was feeling so alone already, and he hadn't even left yet.

About two weeks later Norman sent a telegram indicating that he would be leaving in a few days, but wanted me to meet him in Regensburg to make arrangements for a possible immigration to the U.S. He had urgd me to consider this and wanted to try to help the girls and me to cross the ocean. All plans were halted, however when I received another telegram that said he was leaving the next day. "Will be seeing you again," it said. "You will hear from me soon."

Not until he was really gone did I think about the friend I had lost. We hadn't really had much chance to say goodbye or to talk things over. I hadn't had much opportunity to express my gratitude for all that he had done. I didn't know if we would ever meet again.

At the end of February I received another call from the employment office. The army was establishing a telephone exchange at the regimental headquarters, and civilians were to be hired. Several of us English-speaking women were sent to try our skill at the job, and after a lengthy interview I was one of those hired.

For a week we were trained and then came a period of probation. A few women were then rejected and the rest stayed on. I was lucky this time.

I had to hire someone to care for the children while I was away working. It was difficult to find someone suitable, to say the least. The first one was dishonest; one was pregnant and had to be in confinement all too soon; one was not reliable and went out on errands leaving the children alone; one was a young girl with a skin disease which she passed on to the children. It was an acute case of scabies. A fifth woman brought men into the house and then succeeded in stealing some of my clothes before she quit.

There were months when I didn't have any child care. I was determined not to lose my job, however, and kept hoping that it would work out. Leaving the children unguarded at night was a frightening experience. I can still see Regine crying as I left the room and closed the door.

It was while I was away at work one day that Regine said her first word. I returned home to find Oma chuckling happily over Regine's attempt. She had toddled over to get a dried prune from Oma and reached up with her little hand and said "Danke," which means thank you. I had hoped her first word would be mama, of course, but it was wonderful that she had finally communicated with words! But my little Christel was not the lovely pink baby I wanted her to be, and she looked very weak. People who saw her shook their heads and said: "That child is ill."

In the beginning of March, Schwester Eugenie became so ill that she had to be taken to the hospital. A blood vessel had burst in one of her legs and when I ran into the room I found her in a pool of blood. I quickly tied a piece of cloth tightly above her knee and propped her leg up against the back of a chair. Then I ran out to look for help.

One day, while I was visiting her at the hospital, Oma

had an accident. She couldn't stand on her feet without help, but had tried to hobble with her cane to the bathroom alone. After she went into the room and locked the door, she lost her balance and fell down onto the cement floor, unable to move. Two hours later when I returned from the hospital, I looked for Oma and began to get suspicious when I couldn't find her. I tried the bathroom door and found it locked. Then I heard noises inside and realized what was wrong. I ran to the street looking for help and found a soldier who came with me and worked on the door until the lock came apart. There was Oma lying on the cold floor whimpering quietly. I helped her up and put her to bed. She had a bleeding cut on her forehead and was shivering with cold. I covered her up with a blanket and ran for the doctor. As it turned out, however, she wasn't seriously hurt. Oma didn't have to go to a hospital, but she spent many days in her bed complaining of pain.

Everything at work went relatively well and I grew more and more comfortable with the language I was using, not having spoken much English in the past. There were a couple of incidents that caused a certain amount of humiliation at work, but with the help of my supervisors I was vindicated and, I was able to stay on at the job. I was happy to have a regular income and knew that the loss of my job would have meant a great deal of suffering and more deprivation. The support of a few friends had saved me. Maybe things were looking up again, I said to myself. I must be optimistic in order to survive. Maybe there will be a day when I can go back to Finland and get Harri. My homeland was still behind a wall that separated us, and no communication was possible. I was lonesome for my son and for my childhood home and for my mother. But I would never return empty handed. Oh no, because I could still hear the words my stepfather said: "You have nothing to offer your child." But I was determined to make it some day.

CHAPTER 39
Regine and Christel

Later in the spring both of the children fell ill with the measles. I was without a helper at the time and couldn't get another. Work was a hardship because I lost so much sleep while working at night and caring for the children during the day. Regine recovered comparatively soon because she was the stronger. But Christel didn't seem to get much better. The scarcity of food was at its worst, and I couldn't get what she needed.

Day by day the poor little baby wasted away. Her skin was yellowish and her flesh sagging. Her spine was high and her chest sunken. Her stomach swelled and became abnormally large, although with the doctor's help I fed her the best nourishment I could find.

When I arrived home from work one day I noticed that her eyes were rolling around and shrill cries came from the throat. Picking her up immediately I carried her to the doctor's office. My heart was in my mouth and I sobbed and prayed out loud as I ran.

The waiting room was full of people. I sat down on a corner bench to wait, tears pouring down my cheeks all the while. I couldn't hear or see anything of what was going on around me. I only saw and felt the baby in my lap and heard its shrill cries. She seemed unconscious and her head hung limply down.

People finally alerted the doctors and he came out of his office, took one look at her and ordered me to take her at once to the hospital. There was no time to lose, he said, for she was evidently dying.

I ran now as fast as I could, to the only children's hospital in the city, about a mile and a half away. Oh, those immeasurably long streets! How endless they seemed as I hurried on! People on the street stopped to look at me as I rushed past them, sobbing and crying out. The load was heavy. It was the heaviest and dearest load of my life.

At last at the hospital, I laid the baby down on the emergency table. The doctor took one look at her purple face and rolling eyes and shook his head. "I can't do much for this child. You mothers bring your children to the hospital to die when they are suffering from malnutrition. Why don't you let them die at home? We can't help them when there is no medicine, no food."

No words to express my feelings. I listened to him with a heart as cold as ice. The doctor looked at me and then gave instructions to the nurse. I heard him mention intravenous injections. They took her away from me. With aching arms and an empty feeling in the pit of my stomach I returned home, though I don't remember how. All tears were spent.

Every day I contacted the hospital and learned that Christel still breathed. They didn't let me see her for two weeks. I went to work every day, putting every free moment into prayer. Oma cried with me, for she too loved my baby very much. Sorrow brings friends ever closer together.

Finally our prayers were answered. After two weeks in the hospital little Christel was so much better that I was able to take her home. Some other child needed the bed. The immediate danger was passed and I eagerly went to get her. The poor girl was so small and thin, and her eyes were hollow, and her cheeks sunken. For many days she couldn't raise her head. But slowly she began to improve and my hopes rose with each passing day.

I continued to administer medications to Christel each day but it was difficult to aquire the necessary medicine, and expensive as well. By chance I received help in this regard when I last expected it.

I was in the large mess hall getting my free meal after work one morning and stood looking for a place to sit. About twenty long tables were already full of civilian employees, and a vacant seat was hard to find.

"Vikki, here is an empty chair," I heard a voice calling, and I turned around to see who was calling me. A girl from our exchange motioned to me to come and sit beside her. She introduced her neighbor to me as Mr. Moritz, a very tall and handsome man. I sat down and we talked politely and I was telling him about my children. I mentioned to him about Christel's illness and that I had a very hard time finding medicine for her. Mr. Moritz spoke up then and said he might be able to help since he knew someone who worked for a druggist. I thanked him very much for trying to help and said: "It has been difficult to take care of my children in these circumstances but I would never want to live without them. They are all I have." Mr. Moritz looked at me admiringly and said: "I honor your courage and optimism, and I'll surely do my best to try to help you."

Mr. Moritz kept his promise. The following evening he came to our house and took down the names of the drugs needed. Seeing the conditions under which we were living shocked him. "If my cousin only had known about this before, she certainly would have been ready to help you," he declared. Then he went on telling about his wife and her suicide, brought on by the rigors of the war. Mr. Moritz was left alone with two small children and came to Bayreuth to live with his cousin who now was a loving substitute mother for his children.

A few days later our benefactor, Mr. Moritz, came again carrying a big bag of used clothing. He had told his cousin of our plight and she had gathered a lot of outgrown clothes for my girls. At the same time came medicine from the drugstore. I was very grateful for the gifts and went with Mr. Moritz to his cousin's home to thank her. A friendship grew between us that lasted to the very end of my stay in Bayreuth.

We made memorable hiking trips to the outskirts of the

city and I learned to recognize and know many historically important places in Bayreuth.

Later, when the Richard Wagner Festspielhouse opened its doors to the public, I had the opportunity to enjoy some of the concerts there. In that world-famous opera house, where before the war only Europe's finest productions were presented, still remained a feeling for true art. The presentations which I experienced could not compete with the splendor of old, but the music still lived—was King. God grant that the musical art that once held its head above all others would always keep its proper place in history. Perhaps in time it would unite all the peoples of the world who realize that "Life is short at best and we should be working for the benefit of all."

For many difficult years I wasn't able to enjoy classical music—there was none—or have a chance to play the piano or perform. My life had been too intense. I had been numb for anything else except mere existence. But now, after all those trying years, I was starting to wake up into reality and enjoy one of life's great gifts—Music. Again, like so many times before, it touched the sensitive springs of my soul and left it ringing long after the sound was gone. It was heavenly!

The American soldiers living in our building were mostly very friendly. They loved chidren and many of them came often to our "off-limits" quarters for a chat and to play with my girls. At first we were somewhat hesitant to let them stay and play, but soon we all became used to their friendly ways.

One or two soldiers fell in love with my little Regine, then a two-year-old, lively charmer, and they started bringing her candy and small favors. I was even asked to give Regine up for adoption. Christel was at the time so frail and sick looking that they left her alone.

One of the soldiers, named Bob, was a handsome and intelligent man who was married but had no children. He urged me several times to allow him to adopt Regine and offered 10,000 Marks for her. He came almost every day for a while and played with her. And he told me in rosy detail what a future she could have in America. Of course, I could have used the money for Christel's medical care. But I wouldn't even consider giving up one of my children for any money or promises in the world. I had lost one child and I would never make the same mistake again. Never!

Bob was not satisfied with my refusal and offered fifteen thousand Marks. But I had made up my mind and would not give in. When he left Germany to return to America, Oma was worried stiff that he might come and kidnap Regine when our backs were turned. She locked the doors and checked the windows to make sure that no one could come in uninvited.

One day a very shocking but timely scene met my eyes. Sitting beside a window looking out, I saw through the shrubs and bushes along a path a black soldier and behind him a young German girl, about fourteen, approach. They stopped in a small, grassy spot which was protected from all sides. They apparently felt they could not be seen. My curiosity grew and I watched a digusting scene in front of my eyes. I didn't hear their conversation, but the soldier pointed toward the ground and the girl without hesitation removed her clothing and lay down on the ground. Then he proceeded to undress himself and lay down next to her. After a quick sex act the soldier got up, dressed, gave the girl a candy bar and disappeared into the bushes. A little ashamed, the girl put on her clothes and started in the opposite direction, chewing hungrily on the candy she had earned. A shame boiled inside of me. It was like an animal act, a disgusting example of a sex sale.

CHAPTER 40
A Proposal

Many weeks had passed since Norman had left Europe. There was still no civilian mail service, so we could not communicate directy with each other.

In the middle of May, an American soldier came to our house to deliver a note which he had received from Michigan in a letter addressed to him. The note was for me and it was from Norman.

That note was to change all of my future plans, for it contained a question which read as follows: "There is only one sure way to assure your and the children's future, and that is marriage with me. Think about it and let me know through 'army mail' what your decision is. I love you! Norman."

It came as a surprise, although I had sensed that he liked me a lot, but there it was, a plain and simple proposal.

The matter was on the scales from then on, and we all discussed the proposal thoroughly in our family circle. Oma and Schwester Eugenie were definitely on Norman's side and both advised me to answer in the affirmative immediately, but it wasn't that easy for me to take that step. I had hoped to go back to Finland some day, after I was on my feet again and could afford it. I didn't want to enter my fatherland as a black sheep, with two children and no money, to face my stepfather, but I was waiting for the day when I could stand on Finnish soil again and start a new life with my three children. This time I would be ready to fight for my rights and stepfather's dominating hand would not touch me.

What the future had in store for us—nobody knew.

But what should I do? Should I change my plans and start all over in a new land? Should I completely forget my past? Rolph was gone. I had learned to accept that. I would never forget him, but I had to go on living, to bring up our children and give them the best possible future. I was sure Rolph would want it that way.

I thought about my relationship with Norman. We were very good friends. I knew him well enough to know that he was an honest man and would be a good father for my children. He was quiet and soft spoken and easy to get along with. And, I had felt a great deal of warmth from him. I knew he cared. I felt comfortable with him.

If I decided to accept his offer, I would be able to give my children a home immediately. And I could write to my Aunt Anne and ask her to escort Harri to America, as she had offered to do so many years ago. My family would be together and secure in a new home.

I sent my answer the same way I had received his proposal. I would be happy to accept his offer and was anxious to start the preparations. As soon as the necessary papers were in order, I would meet him in America.

It was very hard to arrange for all of the documents by mail. And unfortunately, the American Consulate, where I had to go to get my visas, was in Munich. It was a long way to travel under existing circumstances. It was going to be a long process, I could tell.

First I went to Munich to find out what papers would be required. I took an early morning train, leaving the children with a nurse. When I arrived there, I had a few hours before the consulate office would open, so I decided to look for the next night's lodgings.

The only person I knew in that large city was Wowa. I didn't have his address, but got it from the police station. Of course, Wowa was ready to help me but he had no place of his own, so he turned to his landlord. The only room available already had eight people sleeping in it, but the refugee family there was willing to take me in for one night.

There was a long line at the consulate. A group of us

were sent into a different room. We were the G.I. brides. There were about ten of us girls, some had or were expecting babies, and we were all anxious to get over to the waiting fathers or future husbands in America. It was an interminable wait. And we filled out form after form.

After a short interview with a clerk, I was told I would have to wait until my papers, which Norman had sent, were found. I sat down to wait. And I waited and waited. After two hours the clerk came to me and asked: "What are you waiting for? Oh, yes, those papers. I will go and look for them now."

Then a little while later she appeared and said that the papers had not been located and that I should go home and wait for a notice to come back again. I returned to Bayreuth emptyhanded. I would have to go on with life as usual and try to wait it out patiently.

Christmas arrived and I planned to have a celebration. Early on Christmas Eve morning, before leaving for work, I trimmed the little tree I had bought and set it in a crock. I filled the crock with coal to help keep it upright, and I put Oma's white cloth on the table under it and cleaned the room for the evening's festivities.

I was without a baby-sitter, so I had to lock the children in. Schwester Eugenie had to care for Oma that day and had to be free to run errands that involved standing in long lines for hours, so she couldn't take care of the children. I had no choice. I planned my day so that I left them dry and fed at seven in the morning and returned to care for them at noon, and again at 3 P.M.

It was dark outside at five o'clock on Christmas Eve as I ran home eagerly through the small path between some old warehouses, to take care of my children and spend the evening with them and friends.

"Hey! Stop! I want to talk to you, Fraulein!" I heard a loud man's voice shouting at me.

I didn't see anybody until suddenly a black figure staggered toward me and grabbed me by my wrist and pulled me to him. It was a black soldier, full of booze who then belched out his insane words: "I love you—I want to kiss you and screw you!"

I tried to get loose from his tight grip, but he pulled me by the hair and brutally pushed me toward a wooden fence nearby, pinning me against it and began to kiss me. This was a terrible nightmare. He was like a wild animal, so excited, so demanding, and his mouth was full of the foul smell of alcohol as he pressed himself against me. I fought him desperately. I kicked and scratched his face and hit him with my fist until we both staggered sideways and fell to the ground between some scratchy bushes.

I could not see his face, he was on top of me and started to rip off my clothes. He was out of his mind. I was panting and shaking for fear and pushed and slapped him frantically. This was like a combat battle and I was very frightened.

But once again my guardian angel was with me. As the man and I rolled around he turned too far to one side trying to remove my pants, and this gave me an opportunity to give him a jerk. He lost his balance for a second. That was enough for me to slide away from his embrace, scramble to my feet, and run. I was shaking with emotion but able to rush into the dark night and disappear. In the distance I could hear his footsteps behind me and his drunken curses calling me back: "I want to screw you. . . ."

Arriving home, I opened the door quietly so I wouldn't awaken my children. What a sight met my eyes! All around the crib where the children stayed there was a ring of black coal dust. The tree had been pulled down and its trimmings torn to pieces. The bed and the once white tablecloth were black from soot, and my colorful American candles had been chewed to bits. And in the midst of it all, the children were sound asleep, looking like two chimney sweeps. But after what I had gone through that day, I didn't mind the mess. I was thankful that they were alive.

It was late at night before I was ready for any celebrating, the cleaning had to be done all over again. But our little family had a small but pleasant meal and a few short moments of prayer. I had to be up early the next morning to get to work by seven.

The real spirit of Christmas was hard to find, though we tried.

In January I received another summons to the consulate in Munich. The ground was frosty and the cold wind howled around the corners when I started my trip. The trains were unheated and I nearly froze all the way there, in spite of the warm clothing I had received from America.

I had no place to spend the night, so I decided to go to the consulate first and apply for my visa. I was able to do so, but was told that it would take about three months before I could hope to leave for America. I should report again in February, the clerk advised, in order that both of the children get their physical examinations.

A friend, Rita, and Wowa were waiting for me at his apartment when I returned from the consulate. All three of us roamed the streets looking for a place for me to stay. It was getting dark and we still had found no place. We were just tired enough to be slightly hysterical, and every little thing amused us out of all proportion.

"Ha," cried Wowa suddenly, as he stopped before a theater poster. "We will see this ballet." And stepping up to the window, he asked for three tickets.

"Sold out," droned the ticket-seller.

Over to one side Rita whispered to me, "Can he afford that?"

"He sure can," I whispered back. "He is working for the American secret service."

Rita was round-eyed with delight.

"Never mind, Wowa," Rita called. "We'll find something else to do." We walked along a short distance and I sighed. I would have enjoyed seeing that ballet. Wowa stood still and snapped his fingers.

"I'll get those tickets," he said as if reading my mind. We went back and he disappeared into the manager's officer. Before long he came out proudly waving three tickets in his hand. Then we hurried away out of sight and amidst laughter that bordered on tears, we asked him how he did it.

"I am now a ballet master and you are touring students. Naturally they want to look out for their co-artists." We were still giggling as we took our seats an hour later.

The results of that Munich trip were good and bad. They were good because I was able to share a few good hours with some close friends before leaving them forever. Those hours were like bright stars in a dark sky. I enjoyed them and remembered them for years, because there were so few during that darkest period in my life.

The bad result of the trip was that I had frozen both of my knees so badly that they became swollen and discolored. I used some unsuitable salve on them and a skin infection spread all over my body, resulting in severe itching and burning. Fortunately I had some help with the children. She was a fifteen-year-old girl, Bertha, who took good care of them which was great relief to me during the two weeks I was incapacitated. A good friend had saved my job during those two weeks by working my shift until I was able to return.

In February I took the children to Munich for their physical exams. Bertha went along to assist me. I was worried about Christel's health. I had been informed that those who failed to pass the physical exam would not be permitted to leave for the U.S. Regine passed her tests with flying colors, but when it was Christel's turn the doctor examined her heart, shook his head and then turned to me and said: "Your child has a heart murmur, malnutrition and rickets. She would probably not survive a boat trip, but I would let her fly. However, when you get to the U.S. be sure to get help immediately for her." I was relieved. . . . We could leave.

CHAPTER 41
A Friend from the Past

As I stood in line for my last x-ray, the girl in front of me turned around, stared at me several times and exclaimed: "Vikki! No. It can't be true?" It was Eva, a college classmate of mine from Sibelius Academi.

"Why, Eva," I cried, "The last time I saw you was in Finland, on our graduation day when you won the scholarship. Did you accept it?"

Eva smiled. "Yes, I was foolish enough to believe that I could go to Munich to study oratorio and Lieder, and be untouched by the war. It was all right for a year, but when I tried to return to Finland I wasn't allowed to and I had to stay here in Munich." You can imagine how it feels to find an old friend in a foreign country!

I told her of my similar experiences and then asked: "What did you do when you found out you couldn't go home?"

"I found work singing on the radio and in churches, and gave voice lessons in my teacher's studio. He was so kind and sympathetic. He and his wife gave me a room and he continued to teach me, although I could no longer pay."

"Are you engaged or married to an American?" I asked.

Eva smiled happily: "Engaged. I met him when I sang for an officers' club in Munich. That was a grand time for me and the audience was the best. But here, in my little locket is the picture of my fiancé, isn't he handsome?" She opened the locket and I agreed.

"We will be living in Kansas City. Oh, I can hardly wait. And you will have to come and visit us!"

But as it turned out, Eva had to wait almost a year before her papers were in order and she could get to America.

At last all reports were okay and we were accepted. I was told to come without the children next time to receive the papers.

I made a couple more trips to Munich before our papers were all in order, however. There was a mix-up that delayed matters for six weeks, but in the end we had everything we needed.

In the meantime, the exchange where I had been working was moved to another city and I was out of work again. I had been offered another position, but as I had hoped to be able to leave soon, I had refused it. Mr. Jansen, always so helpful, wanted to offer me a better position, but I decided against it and began my final preparations for our journey.

Spring was at its loveliest. Beautiful red roses were in full bloom on either side of our street. The city was like a flower garden bursting with color, the air scented with a sweet fragrance. It seemed as if nature was trying to draw her skirts over the ugly scars so recently inflicted by man. I told myself that I would only remember this reborn beauty, for I wanted to remember Europe at its best and not take away with me such a load of bitterness.

The day came when all our papers were in order and I was summoned to the American Consulate for my last interview. The consul was very nice and promised to do all he could to get us on our way before Christel became two years old. There would be a half-fare charge for her if she reached two years and I didn't want Norman to have to pay any more than he had to. We three girls cost him $1000.00 in transportation.

All the tensions and worries were suddenly off of my shoulders and safely wrapped in the big bundle of papers I now carried under my arm as I headed home to Bayreuth.

I sat back in the coach and watched the passing countryside in a relaxed and dispassionate light. I wondered how long it would take for this country to shake off the mantle of misery it had brought upon itself. How long before children warmly dressed and adequately fed, would be running and shouting at play? What would it take to make folks once again smile at strangers, to exchange cheerful greetings, and lend a helping hand?

Back in our little home it didn't take long for me to begin preparing for the trip. As I packed, I talked of my fears and worries, and Oma and Schwester Eugenie tried to reassure me. I was apprehensive about so many things. I hated to arrive in the U.S. empty-handed, with two children for Norman to support. I felt I should at least have something for our new home. Oma saw me brooding and chided me gently.

"Vikki dear, remember you are worth more than objects. With the help and companionship you have to offer, any man you marry cannot help but feel satisfied and go on to a happier life. If Norman loves those children even half as much as I do, his life will be richer for the experience. That is enough."

Oma wiped a tear and whispered, "I love you all very much, and hate to see you go. You are my family now, you know, and my greatest reason for living."

Now it was my turn to comfort Oma. When I thought of all she had done for us, I felt as if I were deserting her. I spoke these thoughts aloud and Oma answered almost angrily.

"No, no. It is selfish to even think of depriving the children of this wonderful opportunity to live a normal life. Besides, you must be very fond of Norman or you wouldn't have accepted his offer."

I hadn't really thought of things that way. But I did feel more at peace with my plan and I realized that I was very happy with Norman. He was gentle, kind and intelligent. And he was the only person since Rolph that I felt I could spend the rest of my life with and be happy. So with my conscience at rest, I went about my packing.

There were small farewell parties. My friends worried about our trip. Did I dare take a plane over the ocean on Friday the thirteenth? That was our date to leave! Wowa arrived from Munich to bid me bon voyage. Good old Wowa who had been ready to help me in almost all of my times of need. While he was in Bayreuth, I introduced him to my girlfriend Marga. They liked each other from the first and later, after I was settled in America, I learned that these two good friends had married. I was very happy for them both.

On the day of departure many friends came to see us off. Schwester Eugenie found willing helpers to carry Oma down to the street level so she could wave goodbye until we were out of sight. I would miss these new-found friends, bound as we were by our common woes. But most of all I would miss Oma and Schwester Eugenie as I would a mother and sister, for that is what they had become to me.

As was to be expected, the train trip was no picnic. It was crowded, the travel was tiring, and children were crying and uncomfortable. But this time there was reason to believe it would be the last trip of this kind. So I held the two babies on my lap and watched the many points of interest fly by. I almost wished that the girls were old enough to understand so I could point things out to them.

See that castle? That is where the great Martin Luther had thrown the ink bottle as he wrestled with the tormentor. This castle, the castle of Wartburg, was used as a sanctuary during the war. And see that river, that is the river Main. There was so much to see and enjoy in Europe.

And I thought of Finland, my fatherland. The country

where everyone works instinctively to make their country strong. Where people are proud of their heritage and where they have a passion for independence which they themselves only know and respect. Perhaps I could have contributed, if I would have returned there.

With a deep sigh I thought of my youth, my family and friends I had left behind. I had no knowledge what changes had taken place during my absence. My homeland was still under the curtain which separated it from the rest of the world. I was leaving a big section of my heart in that little land, but I knew that as soon as I would have Harri by my side in America, I would be happy.

But enough of useless dreaming. Here we were in Frankfurt am Main.

Once more we waited and waited and were pushed and shoved. No wonder the children were tired and cross.

Christel became ill again and was hot with fever complaining of pain in her stomach. I didn't know what else to do so I soothed her as best I could and sang and rocked her to sleep. Then I closed my weary eyes and prayed she would be better soon.

"It's not much longer," I whispered. "Soon everything is going to be all right."

We arrived in Frankfurt two days early because I wanted to be there in plenty of time. I knew that Norman's sister Ruth, who lived in New York, would be waiting for us at the airport. She had promised to take us to her home to wait for Norman's arrival. We had instructions to telephone her from the airport. However, as it turned out, our scheduled flight from Frankfurt to New York was changed. I was encouraged to take a bigger and faster plane to the U.S. because it had more room and it left a day earlier. I was ready to leave any time and felt an earlier flight would be more desirable since our ration cards had run out. I decided to call Ruth immediately upon our arrival to New York.

Before our flight left, we were given a good meal at the airport. That was the first meal I had where one didn't have to worry about ration cards. The children couldn't eat anything, however; they thought the white bread and eggs strange.

The airport was full of passengers running to and fro. Everyone seemed happy and gay, ready to leave the land where the life had been a struggle and burden.

Our flight on Pan American Airways left Europe near midnight. I had to pinch myself to make sure it was all for real. I was so elated I wanted to cry. Were we really going to go to a new land and get a new start?

We made several stops on our flight: London, Ireland, Newfoundland. The children slept most of the trip. I passed my time by talking to some passengers. There were a couple of war brides who couldn't speak English, so I interpreted for them so they could order food, etc.

This was my first flight. The sun shone brightly and its golden ball seemed so near—within reach. The motors were humming steadily. Below us the clouds were like tufts of cotton, soft and fluffy. Here and there I could see the ocean swells glistening in the sun. At the half-way mark we were served coffee with some lovely cakes. Some of the passengers had become afflicted with airsickness and turned their faces away from the tempting food.

The weather was stormier over the Atlantic. There the plane shook and lurched, making long dips now and then. We were flying quite high, above the clouds and the air seemed light and easy to breathe.

Sometimes the sun sent some of her rays to the plane wings which shone like silver, and reflected on the windows so brightly that we had to shade our eyes. Sometimes again we flew through a series of clouds, and I could see thousands of cloud fairies playing around us stroking the windows of the plane with their soft veils, and floating along the back and wings.

While the children slept I sat in thoughts. Europe was far behind now. Before us was a new land with new customs and a new language. Was fate going to smile on us after all the past misery and bitterness? Could I forget it all and begin over again. And how would I be received? It was all so exciting!

I remembered Norman saying to me once before he left that the sun would shine for me again someday. "Someday you will lose that embittered look and be your true, sunny self again." I hoped he was right.

What joy when land was visible. Sighs of relief could be heard all around, and the passengers seemed to brighten up perceptibly.

It was indeed a magnificent land with the scenery changing in rapid succession.

See—over there! Something very tall rising into the sky. And there—and there again. Skyscrapers of course. It was New York in all its immensity and promise.

We were coming into port and we went down at great speed. Another minute, and we could feel the wheels bounce and settle on the ground. America at last!

America. To many Europeans that is a magic word. To thousands of bereft and impoverished people it is truly the promised land where they find inspiration and a chance for a new and better life. America, truly the blessed land of Liberty.

Long live the United States that took us under its wings. Above us the bright blue sky—before us the gate of life through which we would be allowed to enter the happy land.

Joyfully we came, the three of us, for comfort after the many years of bitter experiences. May we sacrifice our strength and love for the land of our dreams. So thinking, we happily disembarked.

Was it—could it be true? To be free in a free land and to start life all over again?

"Dear God," I prayed, make me humble in Thy presence that I may accept this gratefully from Thy goodness and mercy."

CHAPTER 42
The Island of Tears

We didn't leave the plane until we had passed quarantine. Then we were taken to the immigration office to have our passes checked. When it finally came to be our turn the official took the three bundles of papers, one for each of us, and checked them. But he didn't seem to know how to disentangle himself from them. Three different countries of birth and Regine on a Polish quota. He scratched his head and looked at me and then again at the bawling youngsters and finally stated that there must be something wrong with the papers. With red ink he scribbled something over the papers and then disppeared to summon someone to take us away.

After awhile, a tall, uniformed man appeared before me motioning to me to follow. He steered us into a side room and told us to wait. For four long hours we sat and waited and no one came near us.

We were all three of us so tired and hungry and discouraged that I joined the babies and cried. Where were all those wonderful and grateful feelings I had just had a short time before?

Finally someone came and in a surprised tone said: "Oh, you are still here?" We were then taken to an automobile and driven through the city to the docks and then shifted to a freight boat which headed for Ellis Island, the island of tears.

We passed through gates in a great high fence and entered a building, walking down winding corridors. The windows were all covered with iron gratings. We found ourselves finally in a room with a uniformed policeman who locked the door carefully after us. Now we were prisoners behind bars. What a terror!

I can't begin to express my feelings at that time. My thoughts were blacker than black and I would have given anything to have been able to return home to Germany. I had no idea what was going on, or what was going to happen to us.

Then we were led through a large hall to a room where beds were jammed close together and some on top of another. These were canvas cots covered with gray blankets. The room was spilling over with people but they made room for us as well. I looked around us.

There were four black girls next to us with their, to us, very unusual braided hairdos. They stared at us and we at them. The babies began to cry in fright. They had never seen black people before and I guessed that they were frightened by the strange faces. On the other side of us was an Italian family with numerous children. They all talked in their native tongue all at once and continuously.

I threw myself and the girls on the cot and burst into hopeless crying. Why hadn't I stayed with Oma? I wasn't the only one crying, however. There were many kindred souls who were as lost as I, and they too shed bitter tears. I could hear sounds of sadness all around the room.

When I was a little calmer, I looked around the room again. I thought I heard dance music. Was it possible? Music on the Island of Tears? I sat up and thought I could see people dancing beyond the open door. It seemed incomprehensible to me. As it turned out there were people who had spent many months there who, in an effort to entertain themselves, created their own music and dance parties. I turned my back on the dancing and tried to sleep. The children tossed about on their cots, finding no rest. Everything was so strange. Poor little things. What had I gotten them into?

In the night we all awoke with stomach cramps. I feared that we might have contracted typhoid fever, as it was said to be going around. Apparently there had been two persons from the same room who were sent to the hospital with typhoid the day before we arrived.

We were called at 6:30 in the morning for breakfast. On that first day on Ellis Island, however, we couldn't eat anything. The surroundings and our stomach ailments spoiled our appetites. But as we became accustommed to the routine, I was quick to jump at the sound of the bell. All occupants were lined up near the door after which a policeman took us down lengthy corridors to a huge mess hall. There we stood in line waiting our turn. We helped ourselves to what we wanted and the meals seemed pretty good and plentiful. There were complaints, to be sure, but it was certainly better than what I was used to. The worst part of mealtime for me was having to stand in line three times in order to get food for the three of us. This made eating time so short for me that the bell rang for everyone to leave, just as I got started. This way I missed many a meal while feeding the children first.

But, as in so many of my times of need, I found someone who was willing to help me. There was one black cook who seemed to feel sorry for me, and as I passed him going back to my room (usually I was the last one to leave), he would give me something to take along. Sometimes he slipped something into the children's hands as well. I was grateful for his kindheartedness.

While sitting on the edge of my cot on the second day, I noticed insects crawling along the blankets. I was horrified to find that lice were everywhere. I took the blanket to the washroom and tried to shake them out, but I couldn't rid the blanket of all of them. Later I saw cockroaches running over the floor. That made me cringe even more. I didn't dare to step off the bed at night after I was told that the floor was thick with them in the dark.

The inhabitants of Ellis Island were a varied lot. There were different reasons for having individuals there. Some had been there for longer than two years. Some were political prisoners, others were illegal aliens. Many of the inmates who found work in the buildings had children who attended school right on the island.

The black girls sleeping near us were going to New York to school. They had arrived in a boat from some island before their scheduled time and were forced to wait on Ellis Island.

A French family had been trying in vain to get permission to enter the United States. They had a ten-year-old girl who showed definite signs of mental illness and there was little hope that she would be permitted to enter. It was pitiful to watch her wild motions and to listen to her gibberish. She often sat under the table with her plate at mealtimes and periodically would give out with the most extraordinary utterances.

Then there was a young Hungarian woman with very black hair and flashing eyes. She was the center of many males eyes, and I think she knew her power of attraction. I thought she swung her hips a bit coquettishly and winked her eye too playfully. She had probably come to New York to meet a boyfriend, but was unable to convince authorities of her sponsor's sincerity and integrity. She was eventually deported.

I met one war bride who was waiting for permission to enter the country. Her six-year-old daughter was a deaf-mute and needed special permits in order to enter. Lawyers and witnesses at public hearing were part of the process of being released. It was a serious business and there didn't seem much chance of slipping through unnoticed.

226

Outside the building in which we stayed there was an enclosure, where at certain hours of the day, we detainees could walk about. Around this yard were other buildings just like the one we occupied, with barred windows, always full of people. Taunts and vulgar remarks emanated all of the time from those buildings. There were always groups of eager looking men pressing their faces to the fence, staring at the women.

Once a day, at noon, mail was distributed in the big hall. That was the most important event of the day. Every occupant was present, hoping to hear his name called. At the same time, names were called out of those whose business would be taken up by the panel of justice. That panel held its hearings in the back building and, although everyone was anxious to have an opportunity to be heard, we all dreaded the hearings.

I listened intently each day as names were called, hoping each time when a name was mispronounced that it was mine. But nothing happened until the third day. A wire arrived from Norman's sister at last.

"Don't worry," it said. "I will come to help you as soon as possible. Love, Ruth."

On the fifth day on the Island, I heard my name called again and a uniformed policeman announced that I was to appear in the hearing room at once with my two children. He asked me about my ability to speak English and said that unless I could speak and make myself understood, I would have to wait longer until an interpreter could be found. I didn't want to wait another day and took a chance on my English.

The three of us were taken down a few long corridors again and through several locked doors before we reached the hearing room and stood before the examiner.

I felt quite alone and tense as I stepped inside that room. Two examiners in uniform and a policeman and a stenographer sat in their places and eyed me with cold, stern glances. I felt like a guilty criminal standing there before them on the stand.

"Do you have a lawyer to represent you?" boomed the voice of the examiner. It took me a second to get a hold of myself and be calm enough to answer.

"No—no sir," I replied. My words echoed throughout the room as if to taunt me.

"Do you wish to have your relatives present at this hearing?" was the next qustion.

"No sir, I have no relatives here, " I said hesitatingly.

Then the cross-examination began, conducted by both examiners. It lasted about one and a half hours, covering a great deal of my past life up to the present and my reason for coming to the U.S. Then I was finally told the reason for our detention at Ellis Island.

The simple fact was that Regine had received a visitor's visa at the Munich consulate and Christel and I were given permanent resident visas. This had happened because the Polish quota, under which Regine was to enter, was filled at the time of our departure, and she could only receive a short-term visa. The matter was to have been quickly corrected at the immigration office. But it wasn't.

The first hearing ended, and we were taken back to our room. I was spiritually and physically exhausted. There was hope now that we would be out of here soon, but I had many sad and bitter feelings that I would take with me.

Before another two days passed we were called in for another hearing. They had another witness. It was Ruth, Norman's sister. We were meeting for the first time, from across the court room, under very depressing circumstances. We were not allowed to speak to each other. Ruth took the oath, and the cross-examination began.

"Who is this girl?" Ruth was asked, and the examiner pointed at me.

"She is my brother's fiancée, Vikki," she answered confidently.

228

"How do you know that," the other examiner asked quickly. "Have you met her before?"

That, of course, was something she couldn't prove.

"I would know her anywhere from pictures and descriptions my brother gave me," she stated.

The cross-examination went on and on, but at last they were finished. The decision was quick and simple. I was an innocent victim of some oversights at the consulate in Munich. I was allowed to enter the United States of America.

We left Ellis Island the same day. Hundreds of unhappy souls were left behind, people without a country. For a long time after leaving the island I could still see those thick walls barring men and women from freedom, and I understood their grief. I knew I wouldn't easily forget the despair I felt while behind those walls.

While riding in her car toward Ruth's home, she explained to me the events of the past few days: On the day we were scheduled to arrive in New York, Ruth and her husband went to the airport. They didn't get a phone call from me, but thought it wiser to meet every plane that arrived from Europe. Everything had been planned to the last detail. Norman had taken a train to Chicago, from Michigan where he lived, to meet the train on which the children and I were to arrive. Ruth had promised to help us to get on the westbound train. At the airport, however, she was told that the plane arriving from Frankfurt, on which we were supposed to be, had crashed. Our names were on the passenger list. Ruth returned home shocked and confused, not knowing what to do. The worst was, what to tell Norman; he was waiting in Chicago. Finally she decided to send him a wire asking him to wait for a couple of days. In the meantime Ruth wanted to find out more details about the plane crash.

The following day she drove again to the airport and, very fortunately, spoke to a Finnish clerk who was aware that we were sent to Ellis Island. This time Ruth sent me a telegram telling me not to worry.

In the meantime Norman, who had no idea what had happened, called Ruth and found out the details, and decided to take a train to New York.

Ruth made several attempts to see me or to talk to me on the phone, but she was refused and was told she could see me at the court hearing in a few days. The day of the hearing seemed years away, but it finally arrived, and we were together at last. The whole confusion had been the fact that we flew one day earlier than scheduled and the records had not been changed.

At Ruth's home we found Norman waiting. He looked so much taller and slimmer in his new, blue suit than I remembered. I guess I hadn't looked at him with the same eyes before. Now for the first time in eighteen months, we saw each other again. How strange it seemed. I felt a mixture of fear and relief, apprehension and joy. However, our mutual joy in the reunion was paramount.

Ruth took over the care of the children for a few hours so that Norman and I could talk and get used to each other. And when Norman took me in his arms—he was shy, awkward, solid—trying to meet my world somehow, his hazel eyes looked at me so sweetly and tenderly. I started to feel at home then. I felt the warmth of his voice, so soft and caring, as he told me about his plans for our future.

"I have built a house for us in Michigan. A nice, comfortable, three-bedroom one, with a garage below, overlooking Portage Lake. There are large maple trees in front of the house and it has room for a garden. You can make it into a little paradise for our children and us."

"Our children." Did I hear it right? I looked at him with surprise and delight, but before I could respond he continued: "Yes, Regine and Christel will be our children because I want to adopt them. I want to be their father."

With tears in my eyes and my voice trembling with emotion, I looked at him, hesitated, and then asked him, "What about Harri?"

"Of course. He belongs to our family." Norman nodded his head and made it sound certain. "We'll find him and bring him here."

I had everything in the world. After the dreadful past I was being offered a home for my children, and a man who promised to love them like his own, and to love me as well. Our home, our children. That was worth more than anything in the world.

CHAPTER 43
In the Land of Freedom

Two days later we boarded a train and were on our way toward Michigan.

How unlike my recent experiences with trains in Europe. These coaches were clean, the people friendly and unhurried. It seemed strange to go hundreds of miles with never a trace of war damage. When we stopped in stations, I studied many types of people of different nationalities and was impressed how well dressed they all were. I didn't see the bent backs and seamed faces of overburdened humanity so commonly seen abroad. And never had I seen so many automobiles! It seemed like every person in the land had one! I hope the people in America realize the great, good fortune they have, and do everything possible to keep it the way it is. If anyone complained amid all this, it would do him good to go to the land I just left and see the expressions of people's faces—the eyes—always grave old eyes, even in young people—they had lost their luster. Or better still, to go into Russian-controlled countries and see that every citizen is a slave.

I thought of my many friends in foreign countries and how happy they would be to have a chance to live in a land which allowed one to utilize talents and abilities without fear of political persecution, and I realized what wrong impressions many Europeans have of the United States. There were extremes of fact and fancy in the tales that were told, and some thought that just being a United States citizen suddenly produced great wealth, although many had sense enough to know that there had to be all kinds of mentalities, characters, ambitions (or lack of them), as in any group, large or small.

It was getting dark. The sun was going down and the summery June heat was cooling down. Norman and I sat on a light brown upholstered corner bench of a coach car each holding a child on his lap. The light was dim and the children were resting comfortably. Regine asleep on the bench with her head on my lap and sickly little Christel cradled in Norman's arms.

We didn't speak but I found myself looking at the man I soon would marry. I was so calm and at peace. Suddenly I remembered my Uncle Hannes, who had volunteered his services as a physician in Africa years ago and was called Zulu thereafter. To me he was a very wise and understanding individual. When I was a young girl he told me to study a man very carefully before getting more involved with him. "Look at his hands and shoes first, Vikki," he said, "if the hands and nails are clean and the shoes polished, he is most likely a gentleman." With this in mind I glanced at Norman. He was looking at Christel in his arms, shy—adoring—a little curious, and as he bent down to wipe the perspiration from her forehead with a napkin, I looked at his hands. They were large and rough from working hard at his father's 360-acre farm, but clean. His shoulders and back were slightly bent over from carrying too heavy loads as a young boy. I noticed his very large feet in his brown country shoes. They looked clumsy but comfortable and belonged to a man who was loyal and warm and was going to be mine. He was indeed a jewel in the rough.

Norman's hand softly stroked Christel's damp brow and as he looked up I saw a tear steal its way from his eye, and he quickly wiped it away. Christel woke up and let out a little cry and Norman, first uneasy, but soon relaxed, quieted her down. How wonderful, he took part in the care of the children. I thanked God for him.

As if in answer to my prayer, I felt a sense of new strength and serenity. I was sure some higher power was guiding our way.

I looked at the man in front of me, took his hand in mine and closed my eyes. I thought of the song I sang with my mother: *"Skiner sol, hördes åskan gå . . ."*

> Whether the sun shines,
> Or thunder rolls,
> So happy I will always be.
> All goes well, I will rejoice
> All goes wrong, 'twill come out right.

Mother was right. Everything did come out right. I felt the tight lines on my face gradually loosening as if giving way to a gentling wonder. This my harbor, the one I had been longing for. See, mother, I am smiling again!